A Flying Start

Outta This World Advice for Young Men

By Cederick W. Tardy II

Library of Congress Control Number: 2012908013

ISBN-13: 978-0-9792301-3-4

Published by Cederick Tardy Enterprises [Publishing] LLC.
www.cedericktardy.com

Disclaimer: This publication contains the opinions and ideas of its author. It is intended to provide helpful and informative material on the subject matter covered. It is sold with the understanding that the author and publisher are not engaged in rendering professional services in this book. If the reader requires special assistance in specific matters, a competent professional should be consulted. The author and publisher specifically disclaim any responsibility for any liability, loss, or risk, personal or otherwise, which is incurred as a consequence, directly or indirectly, of the use and application of any of the contents of this book. The advice contained herein may not be suitable for every situation. The fact that a website, book, or other source has been referred to in this book does not mean that the author or publisher of this book endorses any other past, present, or future materials used by cited sources or organizations.

Contents

Introduction

"By three methods we may learn wisdom: First, by reflection, which is noblest; second, by imitation, which is easiest; and third, by experience, which is the bitterest." — **Confucius**

Throughout my life I've wished someone would give me a book that could point me in the right direction in life's toughest areas. I've read hundreds of books. Many have changed the way I see the world, but I never found that ONE book. Rather than wait for someone else any longer, I decided to attempt to write the book myself so others might find an easier path.

This book takes you on your journey toward an entirely different life from the one you dreamed of before today. I don't claim that this one book answers every question you've ever had about life. I don't claim that after reading this book, you're equipped to lead the free world. But I will say that reading this book can help you to see your family, your future, and your world in a way that you never have before.

This book has three ideas threaded from beginning to end:
1. Respect your life and your family: The Dream Team Concept
2. Think like a leader: The thought patterns of a *young leader*
3. Broaden your outlook of the world: The pursuit of happiness by finding and developing your passion and purpose for life

There's much to learn, but it's important first for you to understand who I am.

Who I Am

My name is Cederick W. Tardy II, named after my father. I was born in Houston, Texas in 1984. I am the founder of the S.T.R.O.N.G. Association, an organization focused on Strengthening, Training, and Redefining Our Next Generation of young leaders. My organization does this through social awareness initiatives, educational materials, and events focused on building strong families.

I'm the author of four books. My first two books, *The Big Payback* and *A Head Start,* were released in 2007. My most recent two books, *The Seven Secrets of Extremely Successful Mothers* and *A Flying Start: Outta This World Advice for Young Men*, were released in 2012. I have a Bachelor's degree in business finance, and I'm a veteran of the United States Navy and Army. But all of that probably means little to you.

To understand who I really am, you must get an idea of where I started.

My parents divorced when I was in second grade, and my mother took full custody of me. I saw my father just about every other weekend, unless there were schedule conflicts.

From second grade through high school graduation, I was a bad kid. I was never a gangster or a murderer. My troubles were with authority. I hated when people told me what to do. I rebelled against everything that someone told me was *right*. I wasn't a dumb kid. I had dreams and goals, but no one could show me how to reach and use my potential.

Rather than figure out how to find my passion and purpose on my own, I went down the route of drugs and wild, reckless weekends and completely blew off school. I passed high school, but I only put about ten percent of my potential into my twelve years of public school. My friends and I thought the lifestyle we chose was cool. We laughed at the nerds, the ROTC students, those in the band, and everyone else who *tried*.

End result? I haven't kept in touch with any of my old friends, but I know after high school I was miserable. My first job showed me I made some terrible decisions along the way.

I graduated high school in 2002 at 17 years old. No one wanted to hire me, and I didn't want to go to college at all. My grandmother, who was the manager of an apartment complex, offered me a job. I took it. My job title: *garbage man*. Hourly wage: $6. At that time, the minimum wage was $5.25, so I was doing well.

I started early on a Monday morning wearing jeans, a long sleeve T-shirt, and boots. I had my gloves and an optimistic attitude. What I really had was no idea this job would teach me some important lessons about my life. I paired with another kid. Our job description was simple: Pick up the trash around the apartment complex and place it in the Dumpster. The city garbage men would only empty the Dumpsters. They would not pick up trash left around the Dumpsters.

This other kid and I walked from bin to bin picking up trash. There was more trash on the ground than in the containers. The people who lived there either didn't understand the concept of "taking out the trash" or really wanted me to work for my $6 an hour. I can remember about 30 minutes in I picked up a heap of putrid, grimy, soggy, and funky trash. As I lifted the first clump, about 50 to 100 roaches scattered from their hiding place, desperately looking for the next dark area they could find—which was my shadow.

I'm terrified of roaches, so I screamed like a girl, dropped the trash, and just about puked my breakfast. I held it in, however, because it would've only been more for us to clean up. This was awful! I can remember thinking I had no idea life was going to get this crappy.

After regaining my composure, I reached down to pick up another clump of trash. This one turned out to be a rain-soaked baby diaper. I picked it up and baby poop literally leaped from the diaper and splattered onto my boots. This time I puked. I think I cried a bit too. The other kid laughed. We almost got into a fight.

I threw off my gloves and quit. I remember cursing at the other kid. I told him something like, "F*** you and this f***ing job!" Then I stomped my way into my grandmother's office. I told her I was resigning as the garbage man.

I was prepared to argue, fight, or say whatever I needed to say, but I was not going back out there in the hot Texas summer sun to pick up any more trash. Looking me square in the eyes, my grandmother burst into laughter. She laughed so hard I thought she would hurt herself. "What the f*** is she laughing at?" I thought to myself. After she wiped her tears, she looked at her watch and saw it was only about 9:30 in the morning. She said, "Well, you lasted longer than I thought you would."

What I did not understand at the time was that my grandmother had no intention of allowing me to spend the rest of my life as her neighborhood trash man. She wanted me to learn a lesson. Within those 30 minutes, I learned that the decisions I made in the past—and will make in the future—directly affect the opportunities that lay in front of me.

When I chose to skip class, skip the SATs, skip career days, skip college days, and basically skip anything that had the potential to positively influence my life, what I was really skipping were opportunities. That's how I ended up picking up trash on Martin Luther King Blvd. as a high school graduate.

From that point forward, my outlook on life changed. I won't lie to you or have you believe I got my stuff together right away. I wasn't always the author of four books or leader of a nonprofit organization. When I was a teenager, my hobbies included smoking weed, getting drunk, and making money by any means necessary. That life got me arrested several times and led to my becoming a trash man.

I still needed some more Life 101 lessons, but I made a few decisions that took me from trash man to businessman. I joined the Navy. I found new friends. I started *educating myself*. And most importantly, I found a relationship with God.

Eight Myths

We learn to believe things about the way the world works from the day we're born. We learn that fire is hot, dogs can bite, and knives are sharp. We learn these types of lessons either from our parents or from experience.

We learn myths the same way. Myths are unproven or false beliefs, traditions, or legends that people believe simply because everyone else does. We learn them either from our parents or from experiences. The only problem is that myths aren't true. Living our lives by these myths can cause us to make poor choices along the way, which is why it's important to address them face-to-face every day. In each chapter, I'll be doing some myth busting.

Below are eight myths many young people have learned that need some light shed on them before we move on to chapter one.

Myth #1: Teenagers are supposed to rebel.

American society believes teenagers are supposed to rebel and not get along with their parents. Consequently, parents tolerate rebellious behavior, and many young people go way too far in their defiance.

Truth: Teenagers and parents can get along and have a wonderful, mutually beneficial relationship. You'll learn how in the following chapters.

Myth #2: Life gets uninteresting as you age.

Depending on who you listen to, you're prone to believe the only option for your adult life is to graduate high school at 18, get a job or start college, work till retirement while raising a family, and then you die.

Truth: You can design your life to be as amazing or dull as you like. Just read on to find out.

Myth #3: School is a waste of time.

People will tell you your textbooks are outdated, your teachers don't care, and your school only cares about funding, not your future.

Truth: School is only a waste of time if you allow it to be. You can get what you need to get out of it and move on. We'll confront this issue.

Myth #4: Going to college and starting a career is the answer.

With the cost of college tuition rising every year, student loan interest rates set to increase, and the lack of high-paying jobs available to college graduates, does going to college and finding a job sound like a *wise* answer to you?

Truth: College is not a waste of time or money if it's in line with your passion and purpose, but there are thousands of other options available for young people. You'll find some within the chapters of this book.

Myth #5: You need to decide on a career before you leave high school.
Listen to your parents and guidance counselors, and they'll lead you to believe you must make up your mind about your future before you're even sure of your options. Since this was their life experience, they think it should be yours.

Truth: The world has changed dramatically in the past 10 years. You no longer need to go to college immediately after high school. You can go to college online while pursuing something more meaningful to you. Or you can choose to forego college for now and generate income in a thousand other ways that do not require a degree. You'll see the multitude of options available within these pages.

Myth #6: In order to make money, you must get a job.
The unlimited income-generating opportunities that exist for you did not exist for your parents, which is why they believe you must get a job to earn money. They tell you to cut grass, wash cars, pick up trash, or work at the grocery store for minimum wage because it will build character.

Truth: Minimum wage is not going to cut it. Following this advice will not allow you to provide for your family in the way you want to. Rather than working 30 hours a week for minimum wage, you could put your time into self-education and income creation. That info is in these pages.

Myth #7: In order to get girls, you have to be the biggest, coolest, flyest, etc.
You can see young men blindly following this myth every day. They try to dress the best, talk the coolest, act the toughest, and show off in every way possible. Their life is a pursuit of women. Some women love them, and some other men wish to emulate them.

Truth: The lifestyle focused on making yourself attractive by acting leaves men old, empty, and lonely when it's all said and done. Most of the cool guys in your high school are bald and fat by their late 20s. The women who like these types of guys are more likely to be unfaithful and weak. You can learn how to attract the right women.

Myth #8: You're too young to make a difference in the world.
For your entire life, people have told you that you were too small, too young, and too inexperienced. If you believe them, you see a boy in the mirror rather than a young leader. Some people carry this myth with them throughout their lives and never develop into real men.

Truth: You can make a dramatic influence on the world at whatever age you are — nine or ninety. Age is just a number. The ideas you have and your willingness to make them a reality are what matters. You have a purpose. You just have to find it.

These eight myths have caused many young men to grow into old men, angry at how their lives turned out. They allowed themselves to be guided by myths and lies rather than truth. I had to overcome these same myths as I matured. Through my development, I learned to see the world as a young leader.

The word *leader* has many definitions. Ask anyone what a leader is, and they might describe something quite different from what you picture in your mind. It's important that we all start this book with the same definition of a *young leader*.

A young leader is someone who has decided at an early age that he or she is going to design a life based on passion and purpose. This passion and purpose usually generates the income needed to sustain financial independence, but it does not have to. Above all, young leaders make self-education, their families, income generation, freedom, happiness, and some level of service for the good of the world their primary focuses in life.

When I mention young leader, I want you to think of a person who is free from the myths of society and lives according to his passion and purpose. This is the ultimate goal of this book for you.

Are You a Young Leader?

Do you think you have what it takes to become a young leader? Can you overcome the myths that have held others back?

As I travel around the country working with young men and women, I try to show them that becoming a young leader is possible. The idea of designing your own education, career, and lifestyle is overwhelming for many people. Just remember: If I can do it, you can do it.

In 2005, I was going through some big trouble in my personal life. Frustrated, I wrote a letter to my mother that explained the way I felt about my childhood. In this letter, I tried my best to explain how I felt she could have done a better job raising me. From this letter, I started writing my first two books and volunteering with families and youth in my local church. This became my passion.

I began educating myself on how to become an author. In 2007, I published my first two books and helped thousands of families around the country understand a better way of raising young men. The book even sold in Africa, Europe, and Australia, of all places. I was able to generate income from my passion and my purpose. I was happy. And even more, I was doing good for others. To this day I still pursue this passion, and despite the challenges of being a writer, I love it more and more every morning I wake up and look ahead to my day.

Young leaders decide that the old-school advice of unquestioningly following your mother's guidance, going to school, obediently following the advice of your teachers, following all of the rules, staying within the lines, getting a degree and a job, having a family, growing old, retiring, and trying to enjoy some small portion of life before they die is a sham.

Young leaders recognize there's a better way. This approach is to work with their mothers to develop a Dream Team, take advantage of school, pursue additional education aligned with a passion and purpose, start a small enterprise or join a movement, travel and experience all you can every day, generate income from passions, invest it wisely, meet the right woman, build a life together that has purpose and meaning, and teach your children and others to do the same.

Is This a Fairy Tale?

To some people reading this book, all of this seems like a fairy tale. To others, this guidance sounds exactly like what they've waited for their whole lives. Let me explain to you how this all works.

The Seven Secrets of Extremely Successful Mothers is my book geared to mothers of sons.

Many authors write books for mothers or children, but rarely do authors write books for mothers and sons. This difference is important. While you're reading this book and learning how to overcome the challenges that young men face in life, your mother is reading a book about building the Dream Team Concept. In *The Seven Secrets*, I explain to your mom how she can communicate with you, help you discover your passions, invest in your future, adjust the way she disciplines you, and so much more.

Expect your mother's entire parenting style to change after she reads *The Seven Secrets*. She will no longer see you as a boy. She's going to see you as a young leader with a purpose. Your family life will improve. I know this because my mother and I have used these principles to improve the way our family functions. Not only has this Dream Team Concept helped my family, it has helped thousands of families around the country redirect where their lives were headed. This book shows you how to get there.

A Flying Start is the book for sons.

It's important to understand exactly what a flying start is. A flying start is a racing start in which the contestants are already in full motion when they cross the starting line. In other words, it means you have an advantage over people who are standing still when the race begins because you're already moving forward. I titled this book *A Flying Start* because it literally gives you an advantage over the other young men you will grow up with who are standing still (living by myths).

This book has eight chapters. Chapter one is about the Dream Team Concept. Chapter two is about the lifestyle of a leader. Chapter three focuses on self-education. Chapter four takes you through your personal development. Chapter five is about careers and income generation. Chapter six discusses money and financial planning. Chapter seven is all about women, sex, and dating. Chapter eight wraps up the book with a discussion about the world, the future, and where we all fit in.

I chose these eight topics because they make up the biggest challenges and hold the greatest opportunities for young leaders. Understanding the how's and why's associated with each subject brings you closer to the day you can look in the mirror and see all the potential you have inside.

I go further than just giving you eight chapters, however. In each chapter you'll find two surprises. The first is an *Action Challenge*. The action challenges are at the end of every chapter. Their purpose is to help you get moving on what you're reading. Reading is good, but getting up and doing something is even better. That is why you'll be urged to complete the challenges at the end of each chapter.

In addition to the challenges, each chapter has a video associated with it. You will need to visit my website at www.cedericktardy.com and enter the *A Flying Start* section to view the chapter videos.

Some people are read-and-write learners, and others learn through audio and visual formats. For this reason, I developed the chapter videos. I recommend watching each video after each chapter rather than reading the entire book and then going back to watch the videos later. Underneath each video, you have an opportunity to speak directly with me. I read every comment that's posted, and I respond to many of the questions personally. You can also comment on other people's posts and see that you're not the only one with questions.

The end goal of all of this — the two books, the action challenges, and the videos — is to help you and your mother overcome the most common issues holding families back from being amazing. There's only one reason why, after reading this book, you and your mother could fail to create a Dream Team — laziness. There's a lot of work ahead of you, but I promise every bit of it will be worth it.

You will see from chapter one that this is not another book about, "Do the right thing. Get good grades. Practice abstinence. Live like a priest." This book is about uncovering truth and overcoming obstacles. I wish you the best of luck. Chapter one, The Dream Team, awaits you on the next page.

Chapter One: The Dream Team

"A dream team is a group whose members are among the most qualified or talented in their particular fields." — **Webster's Dictionary**

This chapter is about mothers and sons working together. In the introduction, I mentioned my parents divorced when I was in the second grade. I lived with my mother primarily from then on.

As far back as I can remember, my mother and I did not get along. It's hard to explain in writing how bad things were. We didn't talk. We didn't spend time together. We didn't see the world the same. My mother was a career woman. She worked long hours, and sometimes more than one job to provide for the two of us. It was normal for me to see my mom for a total of ten minutes a day during the week since she worked so much.

In elementary school, I got in trouble for talking in class or acting out. In junior high, I got in trouble for arguing with teachers, fighting, or pulling off extreme pranks. But in high school, things got out of hand. The pranks, the rebellion, the fighting, and the attitude reached another level. I started drinking, doing all types of drugs, and caring less about school and more about doing whatever else I wanted to do. Not to mention I was selling pills and weed. Eventually, my mother kicked me out of the house. She sent me to live with my father. I got in trouble there, too. No one knew how to get me straight.

I graduated and became a garbage man before I smartened up, quit smoking, and joined the Navy. It wasn't until I was in the Navy that I realized all the mistakes I made as a young man. It wasn't until I had drill sergeants cursing at me, till I was scraping paint and polishing brass, and until I saw the effects of war firsthand that I understood how badly I messed things up.

I fell into some real trouble when I was 19. Things were really going downhill for me. Around that time, I wrote the letter that grew into my first two books, my income-generating passion, and my purpose. It was also at this time my mother and I started working toward loving, respecting, and helping each other.

Why Did It Take So Long?

When I explain our story to other families, they immediately think they can't change until their child is nineteen or twenty either, but this isn't the case. Your family can change today once you understand what's holding you back. Five things were keeping my family from having a better life much sooner:

1. **We avoided the real issue:** The real issue in our family was not my bad behavior or my mother's workaholism. The real issue was that we avoided having open and honest talks with each other about our expectations, needs, and desires for our family and ourselves.

2. **Generational differences:** Because we avoided open and honest communication, we never understood how differently we thought and viewed the world due to our age and life experience differences.

3. **Philosophical differences:** We thought differently about everything from school to house rules. We each had our own ideas of how things should go.

4. **Parenting style:** What I felt was best for my physical, emotional, social, and intellectual development was different from my mother's ideas. We argued about it regularly, which led to the last obstacle.

5. **Lack of forgiveness:** Neither one of us was ready to forgive the other for the mistakes made in the past. This drove us further apart.

The New Approach

The Seven Secrets, the book for mothers, goes into these challenges and obstacles in much greater detail. In that book your mother is learning a far more effective way to communicate with and lead you. Rather than society telling her what's best for you, I'm suggesting that she look at what is best for you as a young leader. She's learning how to find commonality with you to set family goals, rules, and structure. She's learning how to work with you to create a Dream Team.

Most parents believe that young people rebel because of hormones. They believe it's a natural part of growing up, an expression of independence. My goal is to get your mother and you to understand this isn't the case. Expressing independence and behaving badly are completely different things. Independent behavior is positive. Young people wanting more independence begin to take on responsibility and make their parents' lives easier. Young people who scream and yell, lock their doors, and hide their lives from their parents are not independent; they're immature.

Does your behavior show independence or a lack of maturity?

Why Men Get Into Trouble

I believe that most young men, including me, get into trouble because we lack focus. Men are creators. We have a natural urge to build, shape, or in some way develop things with our natural abilities. Whether it's a Lego structure, a computerized army, a neighborhood business, or an invention for spaceflight, many men have an inherent need to create things.

There is an issue, however. Society, our parents included, doesn't see young men as capable of creating things. Rather than nurture our abilities or teach us how to develop our talents, they put us into school for twelve years. In school, we're taught all sorts of rules that go against our natural desires to create. We're taught to get approval before using the restroom, not to speak without raising our hand in class, and so much more. At home our parents treat us in much the same way.

Depending on how strong the natural urge is, young boys begin to act up. There's too much pent-up energy. To express it, we rebel against the authorities in our lives. We start fighting, talking back, and picking on others. We find things to distract us like sports, girls, or video games. Some kids' parents get worried and place their children on medication for attention deficit disorder, and other kids' parents punish them continually in attempt to break their will.

I don't believe over-medicating or punishment is the answer. I believe that finding a passionate purpose for living is the only solution. Inside everyone is the urge to become a leader, to achieve success, and to create a unique identity. Until they're allowed to do those things, these young people find some other way to express themselves, and too often this leads to trouble.

This Dream Team Concept and the entire focus of *The Seven Secrets* and *A Flying Start* are about helping you and your family develop a purpose, something to focus on, so you can grow up to become the most incredible young man possible.

Player's Positions

For the Dream Team to work, you need to understand each person's position.

Coach: Your mother is the coach of the team. She's ultimately responsible for the direction, instruction, and training of the players. Her job is to develop a strategy for the team that's beneficial for every player. Her job is to make sure the players develop their talents to their peak. Her job is to make sure the team wins.

Player: You're the player, the star player, on the team. Your role on the team is to listen to what the coach is telling you, offer input when you can, and, most important, to play your heart out. Your sole focus as a player is to win the game. You learn the strategy the coach sets. You develop your talents daily. And you perform at your best.

If you have brothers and sisters, realize that they are players as well.

The Dream Team in Real Life

The Dream Team Concept is nothing new. Families throughout history worked together to develop rules, structure, and goals that were mutually beneficial for every member. These families are some of the most famous names in this country such as Kraft, Ford, and Rockefeller. In modern times you can see the results of families who worked together. Below are five examples of successful and famous men who said that their mutually supporting relationship with their mothers is a big part of the reason they are successful.

Sean Combs, also known as P-Diddy among many other names he's used along the way, lost his father when he was three years old. His mother worked very hard to provide for the family and supported him throughout his early struggles in his pursuits in music, fashion, and other ventures.

Alex Rodriguez aka A-Rod, the famous New York Yankees shortstop and one of the highest paid baseball players ever, was raised by his single mother. His dad was in the military and had little contact with him. Alex's mother supported him in his early stages as he pursued a baseball career.

Shaquille O'Neal aka Shaq, the retired basketball legend, grew up apart from his father. His mother played an important role throughout his life, even ensuring he graduated from LSU with a bachelor's degree. Now, Dr. Shaq stands as a gigantic role model for up-and-coming athletes.

World-famous cyclist Lance Armstrong grew up without his father. His mother helped him focus on his dreams early in life. His mother went on to write an inspiring book about raising Lance titled *No Mountain High Enough*.

Shawn Carter, more famously known as Jay-Z, was also raised by his single mother. His mother Gloria helped him early on in life in many ways. Most notably, she purchased his first boom box. He later went on to sell more than 50 million records.

There are millions more stories out there of young men whose mothers understood the Team Concept and used it to help their sons to find their passionate purpose. The point is that when families decide to work together, great things can happen.

Creating the Dream Team in Seven Steps

Up until now, we've described what the Dream Team is, but now it's time to discuss the seven steps you need to follow to create it. Your mother has her own list of steps to follow, so don't feel as if I'm throwing you to the wolves.

Step #1: Stop fighting

Tell your mom you don't want to fight anymore. Explain that you understand the team approach is better for the family than wasting time and energy battling each other. This may be hard for you to do, but it's important to tell her, "I don't want to fight anymore."

Step #2: Start dreaming

You and your mother need to begin to develop ideas of what a Dream Team means for your family. Do this separately at first to keep from influencing each other's ideas. Throughout this book your capacity to dream will quadruple. Bring your new ideas to the table.

Step #3: Compare ideas

After you've developed separate ideas, sit down and compare notes. You'll find there are many similarities in what the two of you want. You can also see the differences. These differences are the reason you work against each other. Recognizing them is an important part of overcoming them.

Step #4: Find common ground

After comparing notes, take the time to develop a vision for the family the two of you can agree on. Decide what's best for the team. This way everyone wins.

Step #5: Research opportunities

Think long, medium, short, and immediate-term when developing strategies and goals together. Use the Internet to find opportunities that are in line with your family's dreams.

Step #6: Build a plan

Using the common vision and the opportunities you've researched, begin to build a plan you both agree on. This is the team's game plan. You will follow it daily, so make sure you both agree on it. Put it in writing and keep it visible.

Step #7: Work the plan
    You may need to adjust the plan over time as you learn and develop, but that's okay. The important part is getting started. Work the plan.

Obstacles to the Dream Team Concept

You'll need to overcome these three obstacles:

1. **The Past:** Built up anger and bitterness from the past prevents people from accepting a new future. The only way to move past this obstacle is to forgive each other.

2. **Communication:** Communication is a skill you have to learn. Your mother sees things differently from you. Rather than try to make her see things as you do, it's better to learn how to see things as she does. Once you understand how someone thinks, you can help that person understand how you think. In the next section I give four bonus communication tips.

3. **Fear of Failure:** Many families use excuses such as not having the time or the money it takes to create a Dream Team. Others say they don't know how to find opportunities to help their teams develop. These are all excuses people make so they won't feel so bad if and when their plans don't work out.

Bonus Communication Tips

Communicating is an important piece of the Dream Team concept. You need to understand how to get your ideas heard. You also need to listen to what your mother is saying. This takes skill. Below are four tips to help you in the process.

Tip #1: Start all of your conversations with a clear purpose.
    Learning to start your conversations with a purpose is a tip you can use throughout your life. Before you and your mother have a serious conversation, create a list of items for what the conversation will be about. This keeps you two on track and prevents arguing about unimportant stuff.

Tip #2: Know your material before you present it.

The best way to persuade someone to agree with you is to be sure you know what you're talking about. The only way to know your subject is to study and prepare your talking points before the conversation. Do research on your own about the things most important to you. Understand how, why, when, where, how much, and everything else you can about your subject. Think through and develop answers for all of the possible objections.

Tip #3: Present your material appropriately.

Rather than scream, cry, or argue, learn to present your ideas in a way your mother is most likely to understand. Does your mother learn best by reading, listening, watching, or doing? Talking is not always effective. By developing your presentation in the way she learns, you're more likely to get your point across.

Tip #4: Listen.

The ability to listen is more important than the ability to talk. People are more likely to listen to you if they know you're listening to them. You want to stay quiet when your mother is talking. A good strategy is to repeat her words in your head as she says them. Do not argue or interrupt at all. Just sit quietly and repeat the words she says in your head. This alone will increase your ability to listen significantly.

You can use these four tips at home immediately. These same tips will serve you well in class, with your friends, and in your future relationships.

Dream Teams Need Rules

If you ever played any game or sport you know that rules are essential. Whether you're playing football, poker, or *Call of Duty*, you need rules and order, or else the others will do whatever they want to do, and nothing gets accomplished. The same idea applies to your Dream Team.

In the past, your mother probably set rules, but they're much different from the rules and structure of a family operating like a Dream Team. The first difference in dream team rules is that they focus on creating freedom rather than restrictions. The second difference is that they focus on creating a young leader rather than a follower.

When your mother was a child, her family most likely believed in harsh, constricting family rules. While certain rules are necessary to keep you away from things you have no business doing, the entire rulebook shouldn't be about what you can't do. In *The Seven Secrets* I advise your mother to develop team rules to help you grow into a man rather than treat you like a child until you're 18 and on your own.

There's one concern. If you're currently acting like an irresponsible person, as I was at your age, it will be difficult for your mother to agree to loosen her shackles on you. I can promise you this, however: If you start following my advice, your mother's rules will get much more relaxed. The rulebook may need to start off as controlling, but once you begin to show you understand you're a true young leader, freedom will come. You'll go from having a midnight curfew to spending your summers in foreign countries.

I have three tips for you when it comes to Dream Team rules:

Tip #1: Get involved.
You need to get involved in the rule-making process. In *The Seven Secrets* I suggest your mother develop a team contract. This contract will guide your family. If you want to agree with it, get involved in making it. Come up with ideas that help your mother feel comfortable, secure, and happy. She'll see your efforts and do the same for you. However, if you fight the process and think the whole idea is dumb, you go back to groundings, punishments, threats, arguing, and fighting. You choose.

Tip #2: Don't mess it up.
I don't expect you never to make mistakes again. Everyone makes them. What I do expect is for you to realize this amazing opportunity. Your mother is willing to transform her entire idea of how to raise you. She's implementing strategies to make your life easier. You must recognize this is a gift few young men will get. Don't throw it away. Do everything you can to show your mother you appreciate the risk she's taking on you. Be the star player.

Tip #3: Excel.
There's a big difference between doing enough and doing excellent. Freedom is the result of trust. Excel with the freedom you're given, and more will be given to you.

Family Legacy

As your Dream Team develops, you'll begin to discuss things like estate planning and family legacy. Family legacy, if you aren't familiar with the term, has to do with the history of your family name. Some of the most famous family names in America are the Hiltons, Rockefellers, Fords, Krafts, Kennedys, and Waltons. When you hear their names you know what they're famous for.

Today's average families have no idea how important building a family legacy is. The successful families know. They protect their legacies and treat them with honor and respect. Every decision the family makes takes the legacy into consideration. I believe regular families like yours and mine should consider modeling ourselves after these successful families.

My mother and I decided our family would dedicate itself to helping other families around the country grow stronger through the lessons we teach. When we pass away, we want people to know that's what we stood for.

The legacy is part of the motivation for doing what you do. Your family legacy is what gives the team pride. It's what your team shouts when it breaks from the huddle. What will you and your mother decide to be known for?

Conclusion

Building a Dream Team is possible for you and you mother no matter where your relationship is right now. There are several roadblocks in the way, but you have the steps to overcome each of them. From this day forward, focus on building a team. Remember your other option is fighting each other. Happiness and freedom await you if you follow the advice in this chapter.

So what is your next step?

Visit www.cedericktardy.com and watch Video #1 titled *Dream Team in Progress*. This video is about the questions you want to think about when imagining how your Dream Team operates. Your answers will help you prepare for the plans you will create in the future. Don't forget to leave a comment with your ideas, thoughts, frustrations, challenges, or triumphs. After you watch the video, take on your first Action Challenge.

Action Challenge

Your first action: Create a Dream Team Album based on the ideas you have for your ideal team. You can use any format you like, but since you're going to show this to your mother, I recommend using a format she's most receptive to. If she appreciates cutout magazine pictures on a piece of paper, use that. If she likes PowerPoint presentations, then use that format. Perhaps your mother needs a video. Use what you know will work.

Go online to gather pictures, videos, articles, and ideas to create a presentation that allows your mother to envision your ideas. This approach is more effective than speaking. During a conversation you may forget important points, miscommunicate an idea, or get interrupted. Your presentation doesn't have these issues.

When you and your mother are ready to discuss Dream Team ideas, bring your presentation to the conversation. Ensure you use the four communication tips found earlier in this chapter, especially tip #2 (Know your material).

Bonus Tip

If you aren't good at creating presentations, try using a freelance artist from Fiverr.com at www.fiverr.com. Get your mother's permission if you don't have access to online payment capabilities before you do this. Spending $5 on a good presentation could mean the difference between your ideas being understood or not. If you or a friend is talented enough to create a good album, don't spend the money. Create the presentation on your own.

I look forward to hearing about how your first Action Challenge went. Feel free to send me a message on Facebook. After you've completed chapter one's video and action challenge, move ahead to chapter two. Chapter two is about developing the lifestyle of a young leader.

Chapter Two: The Lifestyle of a Young Leader

"Your time is limited, so don't waste it living someone else's life."
— **Steve Jobs**

Every great family leaves a legacy and so does every great person. This entire book is about developing a lifestyle of happiness in your heart, home, and the future. This chapter is about developing your personal legacy and lifestyle, the lifestyle of a leader.

What Is Lifestyle?

What is lifestyle, and why is it important to you?

Lifestyle is the way you choose to live. It's how you dress, drive, work, eat, play, spend, and think. Lifestyle is a choice. The lifestyle of a leader is about making a choice to be different from the average. Being unique is a lifestyle choice leaders must make. How can you lead if you're part of the herd?

Remember, in this book, a leader is not someone who has throngs of followers or sits at the head of a table in a boardroom. In this book, a leader is someone who has decided at an early age that he's going to design a life based on a passion and a purpose. This passion and purpose usually generates the income needed to sustain financial independence, but it doesn't have to. A leader makes self-education, family, income generation, freedom, happiness, and some level of service for the good of the world their primary focuses in life.

Leaders are confident, intelligent, funny, generous, classy, and independent people. They choose to find their own way. They're far above the average person who thinks only of himself. The leader lifestyle is above average.

Living the lifestyle of a leader is a matter of choice. You choose whether to live by freedom or fear. The sooner you decide to live by this leadership lifestyle, the sooner you're free to believe in yourself and overcome the peer pressures that hold so many young men back.

Do You Have the Authority?

As a preteen or teenager, how much authority do you really have over your lifestyle? Be honest with yourself. Can you really decide what you eat or drive, where you live, or how you spend your days? You may think the answer is no. But is this the truth?

You may believe you have no control over your lifestyle, but you do. This is a myth you must correct before we continue on. Most young men believe their mothers have ultimate authority over how they spend their time, what they eat, and where they go to school, but this isn't exactly true. Remember the story of how I became a trash man? It was the decisions I made that got me there. I learned an important lesson while picking up trash that every young leader has to learn:

Once we have the ability to make decisions,
we are one hundred percent responsible for our lifestyle.

Every decision you make determines your future, which makes you one hundred percent responsible for your lifestyle. A young leader understands he has a way to gain control of his lifestyle while living at home: the Dream Team Concept. Being part of the Dream Team is your way of having more control over your life while in your mother's house. Whether you buy into the Dream Team Concept or not is your choice. You're one hundred percent responsible for that choice and for the amount of effort you put into designing the team rules and family legacy.

Why So Many People Are Depressed

Depression may be described as feeling sad, blue, unhappy, miserable, or down. Most of us feel this way at some point in our lives, but usually only for short periods. Medical reports estimate that around 19 million Americans are truly depressed, meaning they feel sad, unhappy, and miserable every day of their lives. Why? Why is it that so many people feel depressed for so long? Why do most people feel unhappy and down for even short periods of time?

There are multiple reasons why we might feel unhappy. I don't discredit the impact a family emergency can have on the mood, but I believe there's only one reason so many people today are sad. People are avoiding their natural desire to be unique. By doing this, they're inviting depression into their lives. How can you achieve happiness if deep down you know you aren't being yourself?

Depression is especially dangerous for young people because they're already living through the experimental phase of life. The experimental phase starts around twelve and lasts through twenty-three for many young people. During this time is when young men experiment with body art, sex, drugs, alcohol, extreme behaviors, violence, alternative lifestyles, religion, unconventional education, etc.

When people are depressed, experimentation has a greater chance of developing into addiction and exploitation. They feel as if the world is over. Since the world is already over, they give no thought to the future and begin doing really stupid things with and to their bodies and minds. The more people avoid their urges to be unique, the more depressed they become.

The more depressed they become, the more they become addicted to experimentation. This drives them further away from their passion and purpose, which only drives them further into depression. This cycle repeats itself. The only way out is to *find your reason for living.*

It's important for you to remember that from the ages of between twelve and twenty-three, experimentation is normal. It's common for the majority of us to dabble around with body art, sex, drugs, alcohol, extreme behaviors, violence, alternative lifestyles, religion, new cultures, etc. If anyone tells you differently, they're ill-informed. However, during this phase of life, young leaders remember that experimentation is much different from abuse.

While I strongly recommend avoiding drugs (synthetic, illegal, prescription, OTC), underage drinking, extreme or alternative lifestyles, and wild sexually dangerous behaviors, I know many young people will need to explore for themselves. If you're one of these people, remember you're just experimenting. Do not let that way of life become your lifestyle. As a young leader, you have so many more important things to do with your life than get high, get drunk, get STDs, and get arrested. Trust me.

There are two myths that need to be addressed about uniqueness.

Myth #1: People will ridicule you for being different.
Many people, whether they want to admit it or not, avoid developing their own identities because they're afraid of how other people will perceive them. These "others" can be friends, family, parents, teachers, coaches, or just random people in the world. The fear of being an outsider causes people to cover up their true desires.

Myth #2: You must be a rebel.
You don't have to rebel to live the leader lifestyle. Rebellious behavior is quite different from uniqueness. A rebel rises up against an established authority. Someone who's unique overcomes fears. Uniqueness isn't about challenging everything just to be difficult. It's about challenging the things that hold you back.

The Four Things Holding You Back

Looking within is difficult for many people. People wake up every day and lie to themselves. Young leaders can't live this way and expect to find happiness. Be honest with yourself, and you may see that one or more of these four obstacles are holding you back from creating the lifestyle of your dreams.

1. **Family:** The desire for family approval is a heavy ball and chain for many. The problem: Your family is often influenced by traditions, customs, society's opinions, religion, or past experiences that don't relate to your beliefs.

2. **Friends:** For better or for worse, you're the average of the people you spend the most time with. You only go as far as your friends in school performance, social experimenting, bad behaviors, or in your pursuit of success.

3. **Society:** Without realizing it, you can fall victim to what society says is "good enough for you." Your community has a big influence on how you walk, talk, eat, dress, and behave — for

good or bad. Stepping outside of those social norms is difficult, but critical.

4. **Self:** The only real obstacle is you. You decide whether to allow the other three things to hold you back. You can overcome any setback in life when you decide it's worth the effort.

The American Dream

This country was created so people could embrace individualism. The writers of the Declaration of Independence told us that we had the right to "life, liberty, and the pursuit of happiness." Here's how I define those words:

Life: Growth. Development in character, awareness, and personal opinion.

Liberty: Freedom within society from socially or governmentally enforced social norms.

Happiness: Peaceful, content. Freedom from danger.

We have the right to joy, prosperity, opinion, freedom, and success. People in this country are supposed to be healthy, intelligent, likeable, emotionally stable, and free to believe in their choice of religion, politics, or general life opinions.

So why do so many choose to follow the crowd instead?

Consider these two famous scientific social experiments:

The Stanley Milgram Experiment

The Stanley Milgram Experiment, conducted in 1961, was created to explain the Nazi concentration camp horrors of World War II. The experiment aimed at getting an answer to the question: "How long will someone continue to give electric shocks to another person if they are told to do so, even if they thought they could be seriously hurt?" Milgram created an electric "shock generator" with thirty switches. The switches were marked in fifteen volt increments, ranging from fifteen to four hundred fifty volts. Forty subjects (males) were recruited for the test. The subjects were instructed to teach word-pairs to a learner. When the learner made a mistake, the subject was instructed to punish the learner by giving him a shock, fifteen volts higher for each mistake. During the experiment, many subjects showed signs of anxiety. Three of the subjects had "full-blown, uncontrollable seizures." Although most subjects were uncomfortable doing it, all forty conformed to the pressure up to three hundred volts. Twenty-five of the forty continued to give shocks until the maximum level of four hundred fifty volts was reached. Why? Milgram believed it was because of the person's willingness to follow.

The Asch Conformity Experiment

The Asch Experiment, which Solomon Asch conducted in the 1950s, was a famous experiment designed to test how peer pressure to conform would influence the judgment and individuality of a test subject. In the experiment, conducted on many different occasions, eight subjects were seated around a table. Only one participant was actually a genuine subject, and the other seven were actors. Each participant, in turn, was asked to answer a series of simple questions. At first the actors gave correct answers, but over time they started giving incorrect answers. When surrounded by people giving an incorrect answer, slightly less than one-third of the subjects gave an incorrect response to every question, but about seventy-five percent answered at least one question incorrectly. The results showed that peer pressure could have a considerable influence on the subjects' answers.

These two experiments give us an idea of the impact the influence of family, friends, and society can have on our willingness to be unique. It takes being honest and self-aware to see how outside influences can take us far away from our true selves.

Luckily, there are leaders around to show us that being unique is possible. These men listed below have chosen to go against the opinion of society. They did so early in life. Read their stories of how they kept true to their passion and purpose. These are excellent examples of leaders who chose to build lifestyles designed around purpose, passion, fun, excitement, class, generosity, and personal identity.

John Hope Bryant is an amazing leader that many of you have probably never heard of. Currently, he serves President Barack Obama on the President's Advisory Council on Financial Capability. Prior to that Bryant served President George W. Bush as vice chairman of the Advisory Council on Financial Literacy and chairman of the council's Committee on the Under-Served. John Bryant was the first African-American bestselling business author published in mainstream business leadership in the country.

John Hope Bryant is an entrepreneur and the founder of Operation HOPE. Operation HOPE is America's leading nonprofit organization dedicated to financial literacy and economic empowerment. The organization was founded to break down the barrier between the privileged and poor. Today, HOPE operates in seventy U.S. communities, Haiti, and South Africa and has served more than 1.2 million individuals. The organization has more than 12,500 volunteers, 5,000 partners, and has raised or restructured approximately $900 million for the poor and under-served.

John Hope Bryant is an Oprah's Angel award recipient, TIME Magazine 50 Leaders for the Future, and bestselling author. He lives the lifestyle of leadership, class, intelligence, and generosity.

Someone you may be more familiar with is the super-young and super-rich billionaire brain behind the largest online community ever, Facebook, Mark Zuckerberg.

Zuckerberg is someone we can all look up to. His is the real life story of a nerd who grew up to be the boss of everyone. Zuckerberg began using computers and writing software as a child in middle school. His father taught him about computer programming around the age of nine. His life has been like a movie ever since. He dropped out of Harvard and moved to Palo Alto, California, with a group of friends and within a few years built a multibillion dollar company with more than 900 million active users.

He is a multibillionaire in his twenties. Unlike most Americans, he keeps his lifestyle simple. He has chosen to remain true to himself. He still bikes or walks to work every day. His typical wardrobe includes jeans, a zip-up sweater, and flip flops. Zuckerberg donates an incredible amount of money to various charities. In 2010, he signed a promise along with billionaires Bill Gates and Warren Buffett to donate at least half of their wealth over the course of their lifetime. This expression of leadership and generosity has encouraged other wealthy individuals to sign the Giving Pledge.

Zuckerberg is named as one of the 100 Influential People of the World. In 2009, 2010, 2011, and again in 2012, he was named as *Time* magazine's Person of the Year. In 2012, he was named as part of "The All-Time *Time* 100 of All Time." His personal wealth is estimated to be $17.5 billion, and he's one of the world's youngest billionaires.

Sir Richard Branson is an English businessman. He's best known for his Virgin Group of more than 400 companies. His first business venture was a magazine called *Student* that he started at the age of 16. After this venture, he set up an audio record mail-order business. A post office strike forced him to open a chain of record stores, Virgin Records, which later became known as Virgin Megastores. Branson's Virgin brand grew rapidly. He continued to expand and built Virgin Atlantic Airways and expanded the Virgin Records music label before selling it.

What makes Branson so interesting is his adventurous side. He has made numerous world record-breaking attempts. He beat the record for crossing the Atlantic Ocean in a speedboat by two hours. The next year, he crossed the Atlantic in a hot air balloon. Four years later, Branson crossed the Pacific from Japan to Arctic Canada in another balloon, breaking another record. In March 2010, Branson tried for the world record of putting a round of miniature golf in the dark at the Black Light Mini Golf in The Docklands, Melbourne, Australia. He succeeded in getting 41 on the par 45 course.

Branson is the founder or supporter of several globally important nonprofit organizations that include Virgin United, the Carbon War Room, Global Zero, and the Elders. These organizations do amazing work around the world and only represent a small portion of the generosity and class of this ultra-successful unique man. In Branson's latest book, *Screw Business as Usual*, he outlines a business that values both the traditional, profit-focused model and promotes a philosophy of caring for people, communities, and the planet. In my opinion, Branson is one of the most amazing individuals in the world. As I grow in my personal development and lifestyle of leadership, I try to model myself after his philosophy of business and caring.

These are three stories of amazing leaders who started young with passion and unique ideas and are now giving back to the world in their own ways. They decided who they were going to be despite people telling them to think more realistically. What I don't want you to get caught up in is the fact that these men are extremely wealthy. Wealth is not the point. Do not focus on their dollars; focus on their decisions. Each of these men decided to follow his passionate purpose, educate himself outside of the classroom, and design his lifestyle according to who he wanted to be.

You don't need millions or billions of dollars to live the life of a leader. Rather than money alone, focus on being happy with who you are in the morning when you wake up and at night when you go to sleep. Ask any ultra-wealthy person who has gained money by stealing, drug dealing, or something along those lines if they can sleep at night.

It's Not Dollars, It's Decisions

The truth is the average American makes about $45,000 to $55,000 a year. There are wealthy people who spend more than this on birthday gifts for people who aren't even their family. Nevertheless, $45,000 to $55,000 still provides a comfortable living. While this income level may not be your life's premier goal, understand that by generating income of $151 a day, you can make $55,000 a year and live a pretty comfortable life. You can't donate billions to charity, but you can give time, talent, and energy to worthy causes.

You can lead, starting today, by deciding to be *unquestionably you*. Design your life around a passionate purpose. If possible, use that purpose to create financial independence. The three men above show you it's possible.

Seven Tips to Uniqueness

In later chapters, we're going to discuss finances, income generation, self-education, and more, but for now you need to learn what it takes to become a unique individual. Follow these seven steps on your journey away from the crowd:

Uniqueness Tip #1: Believe in yourself.
   Believe in your own ideas, answers, opinions, and directions. Throughout your life, people are going to tell you what they think is the best for you. Do not blindly follow anyone. Do not go with the crowd for fear of standing out. Make your own decisions.

Uniqueness Tip #2: Do things you love.
   Do things you love and truly enjoy doing. You only live once. Live it the way you know you should be. If you're forced to do something you hate but have to do (for example, school, work, etc.), do it well, do it fast, and get back to doing you.

Uniqueness Tip #3: Think, "If so... then what?"
   Leaders are always questioning the way things work. One of these questions is "If so... then what?" Always think about your actions and the impact they have on your future in these terms: "If I do X, then Y will happen." Is Y the outcome you want for your lifestyle?

Uniqueness Tip #4: Control your thoughts/emotions.
   The easiest way to get people to do what you want is to upset them. Once their emotions are out of their control, they are in your control. This applies to you as well. Guard your thoughts and emotions from the negative influences of others by asking yourself, "Why is this person (or source) telling me this?" In addition, you can control your thoughts by choosing which people and sources you allow yourself to listen to.

Uniqueness Tip #5: Always ask, "Why?"
   Taiichi Ohno, who headed Toyota's production system, always told employees to ask "Why?" five times to get to the root of a problem. In the U.S., we're annoyed when people continually ask "Why?" However, asking "Why?" is an important question in your personal development. Always ask "Why?" and if the answer is ever, "Because that's the way things are done," run away.

Uniqueness Tip #6: Plan your time.

Your time is your most precious asset, and you should strive to have as much control over how you spend it as possible. Set goals for your life, your decades, your years, your months, your weeks, and your days. And then make schedules and plans to achieve those yearly, monthly, weekly, and daily goals. Use your time the best you can.

Uniqueness Tip #7: Avoid cliques.

In order to be unique, sometimes you have to accept being by yourself. Realize it won't last forever. There's nothing wrong with belonging to a group, but don't feel you need to join cliques or associate with certain crowds. Be the person you want to be. If that person is associated with a certain group or label, then okay, but don't become the type of person who thinks the group or label makes them who they are. You are not your brand of clothes, your fraternity, or your neighborhood.

Like all good counsel, these seven tips are simple and effective. Follow them, and you will find yourself leading groups rather than being part of them. You will find yourself at the head of the pack rather than stuck in the middle. Follow these seven tips, and you will find yourself happy, which is by far the most important thing you could ever be.

Conclusion

I am glad that you have made it this far in the book. People with your level of self-discipline are more likely to succeed than those who can't finish a book. I encourage you to keep reading with an open mind. Each chapter will take you further into what it means to be a young leader.

Now please watch Video #2 titled *The Character Traits of a Leader* at www.cedericktardy.com. This video will dive a bit deeper into the makings of an individual who can hold true to what he believes in, even when it's against popular opinion.

I want you to think over these three questions:

1. Am I comfortable when I'm alone?

2. If I were walking in a group and everyone went left at an intersection even though the correct way was right, would I go left or right?
3. What's more important to me, happiness or social acceptance? Are both possible together?

There is no right or wrong answer to these questions. These questions are here to help you think about where you stand on the issue of personal identity.

Action Challenge

Action challenge number two is a bit more thought provoking than the first one. This time I want you to do three things:

1. Figure out what the five most important components of lifestyle design are for you. Five examples for me are: (1) the freedom to live where I want, (2) the freedom to work when I want, (3) the freedom and financial means to travel, (4) the freedom to be creative every day, and (5) the ability to use my passion for writing to generate income.

2. Search the Internet for at least three people (men or women, Americans or not) who are living lifestyles similar to what you have just described. You may not find one person who is doing everything on your list. That's okay. You're unique, so it's unlikely you'd find a bunch of people doing exactly what you want to do.

3. Read the biographies of those people from their or other websites. If you find you want to learn more about them, purchase a book of theirs or about them, if available. Look for common storylines such as their educational journey, their daily lifestyle, their thought processes, their personal character, their outlook of giving back, and anything else to help you on your journey.

I look forward to hearing about how your second action challenge went. I encourage you to post your three lifestyle models underneath chapter two's video. Your comments might help some other reader find a biography of a person they never knew existed.

After you have completed chapter two's video and action challenge, move ahead to chapter three. Chapter three is about self-education, traditional schools, and how to make the most of both.

Chapter Three: Is School Worth Your Time?

"All education is self-education. Period. It doesn't matter if you're sitting in a college classroom or a coffee shop. We don't learn anything we don't want to learn." — **Marc and Angel (bloggers at *Marc and Angel Hack Life*)**

If people like Jay-Z, Bill Gates, Mark Zuckerberg, Richard Branson, LeBron James, Kanye West, and Steve Jobs didn't graduate from college, but your teacher or the store manager at your local Abercrombie & Fitch did, why should you?

Billionaires and millionaires… Thousandaires… This question makes a very strong argument that college may not be all it is cracked up to be. This chapter will address this issue and a lot more on the subject of education for young leaders.

What Is Education?

Education is the process by which you gain knowledge. Knowledge is the sum total of everything you learn from life experience, school, and self-teaching. By gaining knowledge, you become more educated.

The purpose of education varies depending on who you ask. For young leaders, becoming educated allows us to understand the world at a higher, faster level. The more we know, the more opportunities we can take advantage of. The ability to learn specific skills allows us to make greater use of the world around us. Education is about gaining freedom, not just good grades.

Looking at the short list of millionaires and billionaires above, it's foolish to think they weren't educated just because they didn't graduate from college. They understand, as you will after reading this chapter, that education, the process by which you gain knowledge, does not take place in school alone.

Myths About Education

I travel around the country speaking to young people at schools, churches, jails, etc. I speak on many topics, but I love to discuss the importance of getting an education. No matter what part of the country I'm in, I see young people struggling with the same four incorrect beliefs about education.

Myth #1: You don't need an education to be successful.
People hear stories about high school and college dropouts who went on to achieve wealth, fame, and success, and they conjure up this wacky idea that education is a waste of time.

Truth: The truth is that every successful person has gained two types of education — formal and street. Formal education has to do with traditional learning from school, books, or coaching. Street smarts have to do with the skills and techniques you pick up from life experience. Street smarts are just as important and sometimes more important than formal education depending on your passion, purpose, or income generator. BUT their benefits are limited by your level of formal education (math, reading, writing, etc.).

Myth #2: A college degree is the key to a good career.
These students are the exact opposite of those from Myth #1. They believe they must get excellent grades in order to get into college to get a degree to get a job and make money. They believe that a piece of paper with a college's name printed on it is their ticket to salvation in this world.

Truth: College graduates earn more than non-college graduates do over the course of a lifetime. Graduates with a master's degree or doctorate earn even more.

However, these statistics focus solely on careers and jobs. In today's ultracompetitive job market, having a four-year degree isn't necessarily enough to set you apart from the other 13 million unemployed people in this country. You need to focus on earning the right degrees from the right schools. In addition, you need to focus on earning certifications and gaining work experience to be competitive.

At the same time, many successful leaders never spent a day in school after high school. These people had a vision and were willing to take the leap. You have to decide which path is best for you.

Myth #3: Only nerds get straight A's.
I see this attitude in schools around the country, but especially in schools that are predominately Black or Mexican. The young people with this attitude think it is cool to do poorly in school. They make fun of kids who try to do better. If those kids can't maintain their uniqueness, they succumb to the peer pressure.

Truth: You don't have to be a nerd or suck up to a teacher to get good grades in school. I didn't learn this lesson until I started college and military schooling. I learned that studying just a little bit, paying attention in class just a little extra, and asking one or two questions during every class put me at the head of my peer group. Of course people hated on me, but to be honest, people are going to hate on your ambition anyway. Why let their opinion of you determine how you behave? Remember Uniqueness Tip #4: Control your thoughts and emotions. What helps young leaders succeed in school is having a bigger purpose than getting an A in a class. This chapter helps you to discover a bigger purpose.

Myth #4: Knowledge is power.
This motto has been thrown around forever. It's false. Knowledge is not power. Knowing everything in the world won't help you one bit. In fact, knowing too much can cause you to be less effective because you may spend too much time calculating, formulating, and going over the facts rather than acting.

Truth: *Applying* knowledge is power. When you can use things you've learned to control your life, your income, and your impact on the world, then you've gained power.

An America Without Education

Try to imagine an America without an educational system. Your ability to talk, read, add, subtract, formulate opinions, and think through ideas would be severely limited. Without your basic education, you wouldn't even be capable of imagining the things you can now. You wouldn't know they existed or know the words to express your desire for them.

People who have little respect for education don't understand that our country's educational system is the reason we can read, write, and think through problems.

Without an educational system, there would be no medicine; no cars; no grocery stores; no phones; no Internet; no clean, fresh water; no hot and cold water; no music; no fashion; no television; no well-built homes; no roads; no video games; no sports. There would be nothing close to what we have in our daily lives.

People can succeed in this country without higher levels of education. You may not need a high school diploma or a college degree to make it, but that's because long before you and I came along, there were many highly educated people setting up this system in which we live. They created things as advanced as the legal and banking systems and as simple as pictures on a menu at McDonald's so you don't have to read to make your order. You can just point at the burger. The person running the register can then press a button that looks exactly like what you pointed at, and in less than five minutes, you can have something to eat.

Educated people set this system up. Because of their efforts long ago, people like Richard Branson and Jay-Z can use their street knowledge to succeed. This point is important to understand as you go further in life.

Lifestyle Designed by Self-Education

Because you and I are fortunate enough to live in America, we can choose to become anything we want to. We can be fast food employees, janitors, teachers, executives, business owners, investors, or astronauts. The choice is truly ours. We can design our lives based on our education and talents.

As good as our educational system is, young leaders must realize that the goals they have are different from those of the school system. If you wanted to start a business as a photographer, do you think you could learn that skill in school? What about starting any business? What about investing? What about becoming an astronaut?

The answer is no.

School can teach you about photography. Economics class can teach you about the stock market. Business school can teach you about corporate business models. Science classes can teach you about space. But the traditional model of school is not designed to make you an expert in any of these areas. You must pursue your own expertise.

Young leaders have to realize that reaching their lifestyle of choice is not the goal of the educational system. School is designed to give you knowledge and some of the tools necessary for a career. However, it's up to each of us to take responsibility for our educational development if we plan to accomplish our dreams.

Leaders' Attitudes about Traditional Education

Leaders have a different outlook on traditional education. We realize that formal education such as high school, college, advanced certifications, and degrees are a necessary evil that we must endure and triumph over. While we may hate going to class every day, we realize there's a larger purpose for our plight, so we battle through the agony. Rather than do just enough to get by, we decide that while we're being subjected to the torture of formal education, we will make the most of it by learning as much as we can, asking every question we have, and putting everything we are taught to use.

Leaders go a step further still. We realize that school is only going to get us so far. We realize that the level to which we educate ourselves will directly influence how successful we become. This mindset has to do with learning skills that we need to achieve our ultimate passion and purpose. And this has little to do with the classroom. Did school teach Richard Branson how to run 300 companies while attempting to break world records, writing bestselling books, and spearheading some of the world's most influential non-profit organizations?

Did Zuckerberg first learn about computer programming from school or from instruction outside of the classroom?

Acquiring the education in the skills you need to succeed is one hundred percent your responsibility. It isn't your mother's, father's, teacher's, or government's responsibility to teach you how to be happy and fulfill your purpose in life. It's yours. Once you figure that out, all those other resources will line up to help you.

My Story

I have always been a fairly smart guy. You wouldn't have known if you met me in high school. I hated school. I hated school with every single cell I had within me. I spent my junior high and high school years fighting, skipping, partying, in in-school suspension, literally suspended, cheating to get by, high all the time (not in junior high), and always in trouble. I didn't care at all. I graduated high school, and my first job was as a garbage man.

After thirty minutes of picking up trash, I decided to get focused. I joined the Navy and with a new attitude for life, I excelled. I was promoted to the rank of E-4 from E-1 quickly (E stands for enlisted and the numbers for pay grades and amounts of responsibility; E-4 is a petty officer or a noncommissioned officer). I started reading a lot on my own about investing and personal finance. With this knowledge, I started day trading and made some money. In one trade, I made more than $17,000 in less than thirty minutes trading Under Armour's IPO (initial public offering).

In my second year in the Navy, I started going to college. At one point, I was going to three different colleges at the same time and taking two to three classes per semester at each college. This allowed me to earn my bachelor's degree in two and a half years. I maintained a 3.66 GPA, which is an A-. At the same time I was writing my first two books.

Later, I joined the Army as an officer. I excelled in every training course both physically and academically. I got bored in my second year and took Six Sigma certification courses (a business management strategy) through Villanova University. In my third year, I took self-education to an even higher level after I started traveling. I began purchasing online training courses to teach me how to improve my business. I used free courses from various sites on the Internet to enhance my knowledge base. In the end, I used all of this self-directed education to build my second business and re-launch my nonprofit organization.

I regret not taking junior high and high school seriously. It would have been so easy. Every day I wake up and imagine what I could've accomplished had I put this same amount of effort into school when I was twelve to eighteen years old. And I'm not just talking about in school but outside the classroom, as well. There were so many things I wanted to learn and be, but instead I spent my time watching television, getting high, and getting in trouble.

Making the Most of High School

I wake up every single day now and try to make up for lost time. Some people tell me I've already caught up or surpassed expectations. I don't agree. One thing you learn from investing, if you haven't already, is the power of *exponential growth*. Exponential growth basically says that an investment's growth rate will rapidly increase over time due to compounding. In an educational sense, this means that the investment we put into our education today has a much higher return than that same level of education completed three or four years later.

You might believe college is not important. You can fight with your mother and teachers on the subject for your entire four years in high school. You can argue with your mentor. You can argue with me, but you cannot argue with me about whether or not you need to get your high school diploma. People who don't graduate from high school struggle because most employers require a GED or diploma. On top of that, the education you get from high school is more than a diploma.

Junior high and high school are about math and English. Those who drop out of high school or graduate without the ability to read, write, and do math well have a hard time in any area of life. Their career options are limited, *and* they lack the basic skills needed to run a small business.

As hard as it may be for you, GO to school. The ability to read, write, and do math are the most basic skills you need to function. Go to school and make the most of every day you have there. Have fun, but remember school is not about being cool, partying, girls, sports, or popularity. For young leaders, school is about getting the basic skills you need and then getting out of there. You have more important things to do with your time and talents.

Young leaders should:

Focus on excelling in class, take as many AP level courses as possible, and graduate with as many additional skills as they can fit into their schedules.

OR

Focus on graduating school early while still excelling. This next section is about how to graduate school early.

Graduating High School Early

I didn't graduate high school early, but I graduated college early, and it wasn't that hard. Since I had a bigger passion and purpose in mind, I had the drive to graduate early. Rather than skipping classes, I focused on skipping semesters. Let me show you how to do it because there's no point spending four years sitting in class if you don't have to.

Step #1: In order to graduate from high school early, you want to discuss your plans with your mother. There are several planning factors you must consider such as financing your additional classes, transportation, etc. Add "Graduating Early" to your lifestyle design album and discuss this option with your mother.

Step #2: Speak with your teachers, counselors, and principals about the possibilities, opportunities, and process in your district. Every district runs a bit differently, so go directly to the people with the answers for specific advice. Discuss your plans with them. Tell them about your lifestyle design ideas and *inspire them* to help you achieve your goals. Above all, don't take "No" for an answer. There's a way.

Step #3: With your mother's and your counselor's help, build a plan to earn the extra credits you need to graduate half a year, a full year, one and a half years, or two years earlier than normal. Explore all options when building this plan. You can choose to take additional courses online, during summer school, at college, or overseas, earn credits through internships, or develop a *combination* of these. Build a plan that allows you to gain the maximum amount of credits possible per year.

Step #4: If you plan to earn additional education after high school, contact the Admissions Office at the college, technical, or vocational school (several of them) that you want to attend. Explain your plans to them to ensure that all your credits are transferable. If they discover problems with your design, ask for help to fix the glitches. Refine your plan with their help.

Step #5: Focus less on high school stuff and more on your goals of graduating early. Work your plan every day. Sure, it's sad to pass up many of your friends and miss out on the social aspects of high school. It may even get lonely, but keep going. Encourage your friends to follow your lead so they can also become young leaders. Make new friends along the way.

Following these five simple steps allows you to graduate high school and get to work on your passion and purpose much sooner than if you waited the full four years. When you consider the exponential growth factor, you can imagine how much farther ahead you'll be just two years after graduating high school early. Your peers will just be starting their sophomore year of college—that is, if they made it into college at all.

If graduating high school early is just not for you, you have another option for excelling in high school. This option includes:

1. Sit in the front row of every class. Sitting in the front row is one simple change that can catapult you from an average student to an A student.

2. Make friends with your teachers. You don't have to kiss their butts, but respect their powerful pens. They have the authority to change your grades if they believe you're trying. Stay after class, talk to them, ask them questions, and show them you care. You'll be surprised at how much teachers will help you excel if you show them you want to.

3. Make friends with everyone smarter than you. If you previously used to pick on these people and call them names, apologize to them. Stand up for them from this day forward. Show them you have a new respect for school and for them. Don't use them; learn with them. *You are the average of the people you spend the most time with.*

4. Get all As. Getting straight A's takes planning and skill. If you understand the teacher's lecturing and testing style, you can alter your learning and test-taking style. When I adopted this attitude, I began earning nothing less than an A-.

High School Alternatives

Traditional high school is not for everyone. Some of you may find you could be much more successful and happier if you were allowed to pursue one of the four high school alternatives below:

Alternative #1: Magnet school
A magnet school is a public school that offers special instruction unavailable elsewhere. It's designed to attract a diverse student body from a wide geographical area. They have specially trained teachers and staff who truly care about the student's wellbeing. In addition to having better teachers, the other students are more motivated than those at a regular public school. Research magnet schools in your area to see if one might make a great addition to your lifestyle design. Join the school's Facebook page and chat with current students about how they like the school compared to a regular high school.

Alternative #2: Technical school
Technical schools focus on preparing students to meet the challenges of the future by providing relevant education in academic, career, and technical proficiency. Tech schools provide education in mostly employment-preparation skills for trained labor, such as welding, culinary arts, automotive repair, and office management. You need to apply to one of these schools. Research technical high schools in your area to see if these are a better fit for you and your lifestyle design. Join their Facebook pages and chat with current students in a program that interests you.

Alternative #3: Online school

An online school teaches courses entirely or primarily through online methods. This is a great option for people who would rather not bother with going to class. If you'd rather go to school while traveling, volunteering abroad, running a business, or working at your own pace, then consider online schooling as an alternative. This is a growing trend across the country and throughout the world. Ensure that the school you want to attend is properly accredited and go for it. Research online high schools to see if this is a better fit for you and your lifestyle design. Join their Facebook page and chat with current students in a program that interests you.

Alternative #4: Study abroad

To study abroad means you get your education in another country. You can find programs online ranging in length from summer study to graduation. Only about one percent of U.S. students choose to study abroad. Other countries have implemented this alternative for several years, which is why they can read, write, speak, and generate income in other countries much easier than the average American. As the world continues to grow more interconnected, studying abroad may become a necessity rather than an alternative. The experiences gained from living and learning in another country will be invaluable — and a lot of fun. Research study abroad programs in your country of choice to see if one of them is a better fit for you and your lifestyle design. Join their Facebook pages and chat with current students in a program and country that interests you.

These are five alternatives from the traditional high school path, including graduating early. Take the time to research your options. You don't have to sit in school hating life for four years. Make the most of your time.

Making the Most of College

According to the Bureau of Labor Statistics, nearly seventy percent of students who graduate from high school immediately enroll in college. While this is a better than working fast food or stocking retail shelves, you must really ask yourself if you're meant to be part of this seventy percent or not.

If college is a major component of your lifestyle design, you should go. But if your passion and purpose don't require earning a four-year degree or higher, then don't waste your time, money, and energy.

If going to college is a must for your lifestyle design, follow these five tips to ensure that you succeed:

Excelling in College Tip #1: Follow the tips on graduating early from the high school section.
  Build a plan with your counselor's help and work the plan. There are numerous ways to earn credits faster. I graduated in two and a half years, not because I was smarter than everyone else, but because I wanted to get on with my life.

Excelling in College Tip #2: Model each teacher's style.
  Study the directions teachers give you. Learn the way your teacher grades and then structure your work to meet his or her expectations. Voila! Straight A's.

Excelling in College Tip #3: Work ahead of the class using the syllabus as your guide.
  Use the syllabus and the school's online portals to find notes and further guidance to help keep you on track. As you're reading and working ahead, take time to dig deeper into your research by studying additional keywords you're not familiar with online.

Excelling in College Tip #4: Use your resources wisely.
  Talk to people who already took the class to get pointers. Also, work with tutors and study groups. And most important, use the professor's office hours to ask questions, make friends, and show him or her how much you care and are eager to pass the class.

Excelling in College Tip #5: Remember your priorities.
  Party when you can fit it in, but only when you can fit it in. Rather than spend your free time and money drinking, spend your free time making money. Use that money to fund travels during breaks

in school or additional credit accumulation. Focus less on partying, alcohol, sex, drugs, and television and more on getting out of there as soon as you can with the highest degree of applicable skills possible.

Follow these five simple steps, and you can blow college out of the water. You can earn your degree in fewer than four years. It's easy if you remember that college is not life and death. You will see people having panic attacks over assignments and projects. As a young leader, you should relax, learn what your teacher wants, and give him or her exactly what's expected. Get your A and move on to the next class.

College Mistakes

College is a place for you to learn and explore the world and yourself. You're supposed to make mistakes. Nevertheless, there are five mistakes you just don't need to make.

College Mistake #1: Putting too much faith in degrees.
The piece of paper you earn after attending school is only as valuable as your ability to apply what you learned. Focus on making the right contacts, earning additional certifications, and gaining valuable work experience versus just getting good grades.

College Mistake #2: Racking up too much debt.
Young people today are racking up massive amounts of debt in college from student loans or poor financial responsibility with credit cards. Fight for scholarships and research alternatives to pay for school. While you're in school, generate income and spend your money wisely.

College Mistake #3: Attending the wrong schools.
Some people attend the wrong schools and waste years and tons of money in the process. By the wrong school, I mean one that is unaccredited or doesn't have a reputation in the field you're studying.

College Mistake #4: Being too socially minded.
Some people spend too much time focused on being social in school and put little attention into mastering the skills they need to excel later in life.

College Mistake #5: Focusing too much on grades.
Some people focus solely on learning material and passing classes. Make social connections across campus through various clubs, organizations, events, and movements. Approach these clubs and new friends as great ways to meet people who can help you achieve the lifestyle or positions you're working so hard to achieve. Too many young people get wrapped up in their grades and forget life is just as much about the people you know as what you know.

College Alternatives

There are several alternatives to going to college. Below you will find a list of six of them.

College Alternative #1: Vocational school
A vocational or technical school is a school in which students learn the skills needed to perform a particular job. They usually last two years or less.

College Alternative #2: Online college
Going to college online allows you to work at your own pace, pursue a career, travel, or start a business while still earning your degree. Ensure the school is accredited. Here's an example: http://www.extension.harvard.edu/degrees-certificates

College Alternative #3: Certifications
A professional certification is earned by passing an examination. It tells the world you're competent to complete a job or task. The right certifications are extremely lucrative. Here's an example: http://www.cisco.com/web/learning/le3/ccie/index.html

College Alternative #4: Internships
Gaining on-the-job training (OJT) through an internship means you agree to trade your labor for free to gain experience. You can create

a network of contacts, gain school credit, or find full-time work through internships.

College Alternative #5: Military
Joining the Army, Air Force, Navy, Marine Corps, or National Guard may be right for you. You can talk with people who are already in via Facebook to get an idea of the lifestyle. Discuss your options with recruiters.

College Alternative #6: Start a business
What better time to make mistakes than as a teenager or in your early twenties? You can live at home, work out of the garage, and eat for free. There are numerous grants available to help fund your ideas and a wealth of online resources to help you get started. Check out this website: http://sprouter.com

These are just six of the alternatives available to you other than college. There are thousands of others, including going straight to the MLB, the NBA, or the NFL if you're an excellent athlete, joining the Olympic Team, or working abroad as an English-speaking tour guide. There are a ton of options. What do you think is best for you?

Self-Education

With so much focus on high school and college, it's easy for people to forget their education is their responsibility. Here are the ins and outs of *self-education* — the most valuable skill for young leaders.

In self-education, you gain knowledge outside of formal schooling. Having the skills to do this appropriately can directly affect the opportunities you can capitalize on in your lifetime. Most people are so used to formal schooling they have a hard time teaching themselves. Here are three common mistakes of the self-education process:

Mistake #1: No plan.
Those who wish to educate themselves must generate some sort of plan — almost like a syllabus. Failing to do so will almost always lead to wasted time and energy as you find yourself reading and studying things you may never use.

Mistake #2: Study things they can't apply.

By studying subjects they cannot use right away, people waste time and energy. Their intention is to learn something now so they can use it months down the line. The problem is they can't remember what they learned months later. They end up having to relearn it.

Mistake #3: Give up.

Self-education is a skill. You can't walk into a library or get on your computer and begin teaching yourself without learning how to do it properly. Many people try to. After a few hours, a few days, or even a few weeks, they get confused, overwhelmed, and frustrated and give up.

There's a much better way. You'll see my personal strategy later, but first I want to introduce you to the self-education strategy of Darren Hardy. Darren Hardy is an entrepreneur, investor, publisher of *Success* magazine, and author of several books. He's lives a successful and fulfilling life, so take his advice to heart.

Hardy's self-education plan is called the *5-3-1 Program*. His advice is to pick a skill you want to master and systematically read the top five books, listen to the top three audio programs, and attend one seminar on the subject. After completing this program, you'll be in the top five to ten percent of your field. I believe in Hardy's approach, but I tweaked it a bit to make it more applicable for young people who may not be able to afford five books, three audio programs, and a seminar.

What Hardy leaves out is the power of the Internet. If there's one thing for you to take away from this book, it's to *learn how to harness the power of the Internet*. There's so much information available online. With a Wi-Fi enabled laptop, smart phone, iPad, tablet, or any other Internet-connecting device, you can learn almost anything, anywhere, anytime, and almost always for free.

Let me show you how to educate yourself online for free. Afterwards, I will share with you a list of websites to get started on.

The Eight-Step Self-Education Program

Step #1: Pick a topic you want to master.

An example from my life is real estate investing, Internet marketing, or writing and selling books.

Step #2: Google the subject you want to master.

Sometimes Google can provide junk resources, so consider using websites like Wikipedia or Wiki-how and then proceed to more authoritative sources.

Step #3: Read.

Read at least three to five articles, PDFs, eBooks, Web pages, blogs, etc. on your subject. Read only the results from within the past year or two, if possible, by adding the year to the end of your search in quotations. Example: "2012"

Step #4: Create a document of everything you don't know to learn more about.

For example, in Internet marketing, I needed to learn more about SEO, Google AdWords, and social media marketing. Even if they are just words you didn't understand while reading during step #3, write them down.

Step #5: Scroll down to the bottom of the source you're reading.

Look for citations and sources. Add those cited sources to your document. If they have hyperlinks, you can look at them now or write them down for later.

Step #6: Search through each of the words, phrases, ideas, and cited resources on your list.

You'll need to expand your document further as you begin to expose yourself to bigger ideas, new words, and things you had no idea existed.

Step #7: Take the top five to ten keywords in your document and learn more about them.

Once you have a good understanding of all of the components that make up the subject you want to master, use these five or ten keywords for further study. Search for videos, tutorials, training, podcasts, and slideshows. For example in real estate investing, I may search for "multiunit property management tutorials" or "property inspection videos." Study everything you can.

Step #8: Use email and social media.

Connect with experts and online communities of people who are already doing what you want to do.

Within three to six months of following this program, you can become highly knowledgeable in any topic. When you have learned all you can for free, then purchase programs, tutoring, coaching, or whatever you need to move up to the next level of training you need.

Problems Staying Focused?

Do you have a hard time staying focused for long periods of time? Is it hard enough for you to finish this book, let alone try to teach yourself? This is normal. I had the same issues. This section will help you understand the problem and the solution.

Many teachers, parents, doctors, and counselors believe that a child who can't sit still and focus in class has ADD or ADHD (attention deficit disorder or attention deficit hyperactivity disorder). The symptoms of these disorders are:

- Difficulty paying attention to details and tendency to make careless mistakes
- Inability to sustain attention on tasks or activities
- Difficulty finishing schoolwork or paperwork or performing tasks that require concentration
- Fidgeting and other restless behavior
- Sometimes irrational outbursts

Rather than look at what the real issues might be, many authority figures recommend prescribing medications such as Adderall, Ritalin, Dexedrine, or Strattera to reduce these undesirable behaviors. I have nothing against using medications if you absolutely need to use them, but I think addressing the real issue is more important. It's important to understand what attention span is.

Attention span is the amount of time a person can concentrate on a task without becoming distracted. How long can you sit and listen to a teacher before you start talking to a friend? How long can you start researching on the Internet before you end up playing games or chatting on Facebook?

Attention span is less about the ability to pay attention and more about what someone is expected to pay attention to. It may be difficult for you to pay attention in high school, but if you attended school abroad, you may find that your attention span increases dramatically. The difference is in how much you care.

Personally, I can only pay attention to something I don't care about for roughly ten to fifteen seconds. After that I get antsy and frustrated and want to slap whoever is behind my suffering. But do I have ADHD? No. Like so many other people, I have IDCAT: It stands for "I Don't Care About This," and it's common for every one of us.

How else do you explain my ability to sit at my computer and research and study and write for sometimes more than fifteen hours a day, while not being able to sit for fifteen seconds in a boring lecture? How do you explain young people's ability to play video games for hours on end, but they can't get through their homework without checking their phone five hundred times?

The point is that not paying attention is not a medical condition; it's a condition of your will. When you find something you love, you can focus on it for days with almost no food, water, or sunlight. No medication and no phones.

If you're having problems focusing,
the cure is finding something you're more interested in.

Conclusion

Self-education or educational lifestyle design is a must for all young leaders. This skill will serve you now and for the rest of your life. Right now, you know more about the process of self-education than most adults do. Go out and use.

Visit www.cedericktardy.com to watch Video #3 titled *Building Your Educational Plan*. This video will walk you through how to build your plan as well as learn how to raise money for additional courses, seminars, study abroad programs, and more.

Action Challenge

This action challenge has three simple steps.
1. Watch Video #3 on building your educational plan.
2. Build an educational plan that's based on your passion.
3. Follow the plan for just 21 days.

You'll be amazed at how much more interesting the world gets.

Additional Resources

Below is a list of some of the best free online educational sources available. Google the phrase to get to the current websites because the names may have changed between the printing of this book and the time you're reading it.

Science
- MIT Open Courseware: MIT Open Courseware is a free Web-based publication of the Massachusetts Institute of Technology's course materials that reflect almost all the undergraduate and graduate subjects taught at MIT.

- How Stuff Works Science: More scientific lessons and explanations than you could sort through for an entire year.

Health
- Harvard Medical School Open Courseware: The mission of the Harvard Medical School Open Courseware Initiative is to share knowledge from the Harvard community of scholars to other academic institutions, prospective students, and the general public.

- Johns Hopkins Open Courseware: The Johns Hopkins Bloomberg School of Public Health's Open Courseware project provides access to content of the school's most popular courses.

Math

- Khan Academy: More than 1,200 video lessons covering everything from basic arithmetic and algebra to differential equations, physics, chemistry, and biology.

- AMSER: AMSER (the Applied Math and Science Education Repository) is a portal of educational resources and services built specifically for use by those in community and technical colleges but free for anyone to use.

- Oxford University Mathematics Open Courseware: Various online mathematics classes provided free by Oxford University in England.

- UMass Boston Mathematics Open Courseware: Various online mathematics classes provided free by the University of Massachusetts in Boston.

Investing and Finance

- Investopedia Financial Investing Tutorials: Detailed lessons on money management and investing.

- The Street University: If you're just starting out as an investor or need a refresher course, this site can help you learn what you need to know.

Business

- MIT Sloan School of Management Open Courseware: MIT Sloan is a world-class business school long renowned for thought leadership and the ability to successfully partner theory and practice.

- My Own Business, Inc: Offers a free online business administration course that covers topics like business plans, accounting, marketing, insurance, e-commerce, and international trade.

History
- University of Washington's OpenUW: Explore a variety of topics in several free history-centric online courses from the University of Washington.

- Notre Dame Open Courseware: Notre Dame OCW is a free and open educational resource for faculty, students, and self-learners throughout the world.

Law
- Duke Law Center for the Public Domain: Duke University is counted among the best schools in the South. If you're interested in law, Duke's open courseware in that subject area can go a long way toward helping you learn more about the justice system.

- Boston College Front Row (Law): Boston College Front Row is a website that offers free access through streaming media to tapes of cultural and scholarly events at Boston College. Click on programs and browse by category.

Computers and Programming
- Wikiversity School of Computer Science and Technology: Wikiversity is a Wikimedia Foundation project devoted to learning resources, learning projects, and research for use in all levels, types, and styles of education from preschool to university, including professional training and informal learning.

- Dream.In.Code Tutorials: Lots of computer programming tutorials.

- FreeTechBooks.com: This site lists free online computer science, engineering, and programming books, textbooks and lecture notes, all of which are legally and freely available over the Internet.

- GCF International: Whether you're new to computers or just want to gain more skills, the free computer tutorials can help. From Computer Basics to Microsoft Office to Apple, there's a wide range of free computer tutorials to choose from.

- How to Program It: Teach yourself computer programming basics with the courses from this website.

English and Writing
- Open Yale Courses (English): Open Yale Courses provides lectures and other materials from selected Yale College courses to the public free of charge via the Internet.

- Guide to Grammar and Writing: Grammar and writing techniques, lessons, and quizzes.

- Purdue Online Writing Lab: More than two hundred free resources, including lessons on writing, research, grammar, and style guides.

Languages
- Mango Languages: More than one hundred lessons, shown to you in PowerPoint style with quizzes to move you through any language without cracking a book.

- BBC Languages: Teach yourself a new spoken language online.

Various
- YouTube EDU: Educational videos on YouTube organized by subject matter.

- LearnHub Test Prep: Raise your test scores with free practice tests and counseling on various subjects.

- iTunes U: Hundreds of universities, including Stanford, Yale and MIT, distribute lectures, slide shows, PDFs, films, exhibit tours, and audio books through iTunes U. The science section alone contains content on topics including agriculture, astronomy, biology, chemistry, physics, ecology, and geography.

- TED: Motivational and educational lectures from noteworthy professionals around the world.

- Scribd: Scribd is an online document sharing site that supports Word, Excel, PowerPoint, PDF, and other popular formats. You can download a document or embed it in your blog or Web page.

Chapter Four: Personal Development Is a Journey

"You don't learn to walk by following rules. You learn by doing and by falling over." — **Richard Branson, entrepreneur (Virgin Group) and adventurer**

This chapter is about developing leaders from the inside out. So much goes into the composition of a leader. There are many examples of men today such as Richard Branson and Bill Gates who live truly amazing lives of passion and purpose. I repeat those two words, *passion* and *purpose*, many times because your long-term happiness relies on you fully developing into the person you were born to be. Developing from the inside out is a lifelong process that starts in the mind.

Leaders think differently from normal people. Leaders have different habits and behave in ways that make average people scratch their heads. Average people are amazed at how two men can have the same traditional schooling and same economic starting point, but one man's results will trounce the other's.

Leaders get different results because they've developed different habits for their personal lives. People like Richard Branson are always thinking ahead. People like Apple's late CEO Steve Jobs are always thinking, "Why? How? Can this be done differently? Can this be done faster? Can this be done better?"

Leaders don't wake up one day and create companies like Apple or Virgin. They develop ideas in their minds and then through intense rounds of self-education bring their ideas into reality. But how? How is it that one computer programmer can hardly develop a basic computer game while another can develop Facebook? What sets the two apart?

The difference in the two is a *mindset*, the mindset of personal development. The mindset that says, "I can develop into anything I want by figuring out how." And not only do you think the thoughts, but you actually build the plans and follow them without quitting until you see yourself in reality where you originally only had dreamed of standing.

The proper mindset separates winners from losers. You can see this early on. Some children get A's and B's while others get C's and below. They have the same teachers, same textbooks, same pencil and paper, but the two groups of children view school differently. The A-B group approaches school with the mindset of mastery. The C-F group approaches school with the mindset of enough to get by.

The issue with the "enough to get by" attitude is that it becomes a habit. It starts with school but eventually creeps into other areas of life: work, family, future planning, etc. The A-B students take their mastery mindset attitude with them, as well. As they grow older, they habitually develop higher standards of living for themselves.

When you first approach people with this idea, they have all sorts of arguments. They refuse to believe they're responsible for their low-level life. It can't be their fault. It must be the Democrats, the Republicans, the immigrants, the teachers, the minorities, the government, the devil, or terrorists! Someone else must be to blame for how poorly their lives have turned out.

Some people refuse to let go of a myth that has kept people down for thousands of years. That myth is: People are born with talents, skills, intelligence, and wisdom, which is why they're more successful than others. This lie has allowed people to have yet another excuse, genetics, for why they will never become successful, passionate, or happy.

The truth is no one is born successful. No one is born on top. We're all born with *potential*. Mark Zuckerberg's parents were regular hardworking people. Tiger Woods didn't come out of the womb winning golf tournaments. LeBron James couldn't dunk as an infant. Richard Branson had trouble passing school due to dyslexia. These people found their passions and put time into developing their skills. They fully embraced the concept of personal development and trusted in the 10,000 Hour Rule, the idea that it takes approximately 10,000 hours of deliberate practice to master a skill.

So before you give up and quit, think about the 10,000 Hour Rule. Have you even put 300 hours into your passion? Have you spent 10,000 hours dribbling, drawing, calculating, programming, investing, or doing whatever your desire is?

High-Level Personal Development

Personal development has several different definitions, depending on whom you talk to. In this book, personal development means improving your mind, body, and spirit with the purpose of enhancing the quality of your life. This means that every day you should focus on improving your brainpower and intelligence, your muscles and health, as well as your character and enthusiasm for life.

How much time have you spent today working on those areas? How about in the past week? How about in the past month? How about your friends? How about your mother? Where does personal development rank in your list of priorities?

For young leaders, personal development should rank fairly high on the priority chart. Creating the habits of thought, communication, and learning that lead to accomplishing your passion and purpose should rank just below eating, breathing, drinking water, and sleeping, in my opinion.

This way of living is referred to as *high-level living*. There are several obstacles in the way of high-level living you must overcome. Basic psychology teaches that in order to reach this level of thinking, you have to first feel safe and secure, have plenty of food and water, and feel loved. For this reason *The Seven Secrets*, the companion book for mothers, goes into great detail about how to make sure these basic needs are met for you and your family.

Some of you may not have all your basic needs met. On the other hand, many of you do and are still not experiencing the benefits of high-level living because you're avoiding the hard work it requires to develop yourself. As covered in chapter three, teaching yourself is difficult. Developing your mind, body, and soul is equally as difficult.

People have a natural tendency to run away from things that are difficult (painful) and toward things that are easier (pleasurable). Some psychologists believe this is an evolutionary adaptation. I disagree to an extent. It's often the most difficult things that bring the greatest rewards. If evolution is about survival of the fittest, wouldn't the trait of facing difficulty be the perfect adaptation to have?

Rather than an evolutionary adaptation, I think we avoid difficulty because we can. We know we don't have to try hard to make it in life. We can get by with just enough. We've done it since grade school, and that habit hasn't gotten us killed yet. It's easier, so we stick with it.

Young leaders think differently.

The Personal Development Journey and Its Evolution

High-level living is a journey toward happiness and ultimate satisfaction with self. A journey. A journey differs from normal commuting from point A to point B. A journey is more like a road trip. It's full of beautiful scenery, gorgeous vistas, and roads you've never traveled before.

No matter what things may look like for you now, it's important to understand that life has much more to offer. Life is more than homework and tests. Life is much more than living to work. And life is much more than living to die eventually. Life is a once-in-a-lifetime gift.

The journey of personal development has many different phases. As I talk with young people around the country, I find it reassuring to explain these phases in detail so they understand they aren't lost, abnormal, or going crazy.

The next section is going to explain the nine phases of the journey so you can know exactly where you are and where you're going. This portion of the book is so important that it's available for download on my website. It may be helpful for you to print out these *Journey Checkpoints* and pin them to your wall as a reminder that everything is okay. You're normal. This is just the way things go.

The Nine Checkpoints Along the Personal Development Journey

Checkpoint #1: It starts with frustration.
You're uncomfortable, depressed, or anxious but can't really figure out why.

Checkpoint #2: You ask yourself seven questions.
1. What am I doing with my life?
2. Am I doing something that matters?
3. Am I ever going to be happy?
4. What do I love to do, and what am I doing about it?
5. Has my life brought joy to others?
6. Am I pursuing my dream, or is fear stopping me?
7. What am I doing to help others?

Checkpoint #3: You begin looking for answers.
You look to books, friends, family, relationships, religion, etc. You do a sincere and thorough search.

Checkpoint #4: You experiment with all sorts of things.
You start trying to find your own way. Some people try new haircuts, new workouts, new hobbies, new girlfriends, or dangerous behaviors. Others go a more positive route with education, travel, volunteering, etc.

Checkpoint #5: You come to a quit or go forward point.
Eventually you come to a point where you decide to answer the seven questions truthfully. Those who do go forward to high-level living. Those who continue to lie to themselves fall into low-level living.

Checkpoint #6: If you go forward, you find your answers.
The moment you decide to be honest with yourself is the moment you start to see the truth in everything else around you.

Checkpoint #7: You give your waking and sleeping moments to those answers.

You can no longer sleep at night because the only thing that matters is the truth — your pursuit toward happiness through passion and purpose.

Checkpoint #8: You succeed or fail.

Rarely is anyone successful every time. Sometimes you win and sometimes you lose, but either way you're happy because you did more than nothing.

Checkpoint #9: Succeed or fail, eventually you grow frustrated again.

Your life is trying to tell you there's still more for you to do. Then, you go back to Checkpoint #1.

This personal development journey is normal. The greatest men tell similar life stories. Read their biographies and autobiographies, and you'll see how they continuously loop through these nine checkpoints.

My Personal Development Story

At the time of writing this book, I'm at checkpoint #7. I love what I'm doing more and more each day. My journey started years ago when I decided I was going to stop lying to myself. I made the decision to start making the most of life by learning new things every day, traveling, enjoying the great outdoors, and generating income from things that made me happy. I am still on this journey.

Not too long ago I was a C-F student living a low-level life, avoiding difficulty and running toward constant pleasure. That mindset became my habit and my ultimate designed lifestyle. Those habits led me to become a garbage man. But I realized my frustration was a signal telling me that life had much more to offer me. I asked myself similar questions to those seven above. Over a period of a few years, I experimented with several answers until I found my true identity or what made me happy. I developed new habits, mastery mindset habits, and those new habits produced a new lifestyle for me.

I have gone up and down in life. I have had to go back to Checkpoint #1 several times, but I never gave up. Some of the things I'm most proud of in my life are the result of my willingness to continue this journey. This is a list of some of the things I've accomplished:

- Published four books
- Earned my bachelor's degree
- Started three legitimate businesses
- Been featured in national and local magazines
- Been featured as a regular guest on a radio show
- Deployed to Afghanistan with the Army
- Deployed twice in the Navy (all over the world)
- Danced the tango in Buenos Aires, Argentina
- Ate and discussed existence with monks in Thailand
- Climbed mountains in Patagonia in South America
- Rode elephants through the jungle
- Flew an airplane (takeoff and landing)
- Dove down to 100 feet to explore a shipwreck
- Dove with sharks and eagle rays in Costa Rica
- Volunteered with single mothers in Mexico
- Fished around the world
- Spoke to crowds of 5,000 young people
- Traded stocks (lost big and won big)
- Managed real estate
- Partied at some of the world's most famous parties
- Skydived from 11,000 feet

There are still probably 1,000 things I have left to do if you include all the places I'd like to visit and people I'd like to meet. Some of the top things on my lifelong to-do list are:

- Climb Mount Everest
- Visit every mega waterfall in the world
- Travel to outer space
- Own and manage a sizeable real estate portfolio
- Visit every country to learn from their leading minds

When I was 18, my biggest dream was to retire from the military and purchase a BMW. The journey expands your thoughts and perceptions of what is possible for you.

How to Develop a Passionate Personality

I'm often asked, "How do you develop into someone who is passionate about life and living with purpose?" It's hard for people to understand that I read, listen to, and watch a lot of different things, and pick up lessons from people I admire such as Richard Branson. Rather than try to explain what works for me, I developed a simple six-step system to help everyone through the process of developing into a passionate person.

Six Steps for Developing a Passionate Personality

1. Decide to create your own unique identity.
2. Become aware of everything. Use your five senses to notice the smallest details.
3. Appreciate being alone and the freedom it gives.
4. Experiment with different ideas and plans until you find what works.
5. Develop your talents in the areas you find most appealing through deliberate study.
6. Work hard.

You can do steps one through five, but without step six, you might as well consider a life of cooking fries or picking up trash.

What Next?

The best conversations are with people who ask, "What do I do next?" These people are thirsty for life. I assume that by reading this far, you're one of those people, so here are five pointers for what to do after you find your passion. These five points are very simple but very effective in creating a happy, well-rounded individual.

1. Educate yourself. If you don't know how to do something, learn how.
2. Take a nap when you're frustrated and can't figure out what to do about a situation.
3. Make and save money to invest in your education and application phases.
4. Work your plan with a "nothing else matters" approach.

5.   Ride the journey through all nine steps without giving up.

"The big secret in life is that there is no big secret. Whatever your goal, you can get there if you're willing to work." — **Oprah Winfrey**

37 More Tips to Help You on Your Journey

You want to read over this section again and again throughout your journey. These are some of the most inspiring pointers on personal development collected from multiple sources.

1.   Live your life as if someone's always watching you.
2.   Realize that solutions you never could have imagined only come after you start.
3.   Set goals for each day the night before. Decide what you'll do; then do it.
4.   Identify your tasks for the next day and set out the materials in advance.
5.   Do your most important work during your peak productivity times.
6.   Allocate uninterruptible blocks of time for solo work when you must concentrate.
7.   Start your days early.
8.   Try to do everything a little faster than usual.
9.   Focus your energy on the twenty percent of things that work and dump the other eighty.
10. Take action immediately after setting a goal.
11. Separate the truly important tasks from the rest.
12. Learn to speed-read.
13. Learn and memorize something new every day.
14. Reduce your attachment to possessions.
15. Develop an endless curiosity about life and the world.
16. Exercise your body.
17. Drink lots of water every day.
18. Don't take life so seriously! Learn to laugh.
19. Read books.
20. Get out in the sun every day.
21. Find your passion and purpose for living.
22. Start your days by doing things that make you smile.

23. Write your problems, concerns, and fears onto paper and burn them.
24. Travel to as many different parts of the world as you can.
25. Don't let other people's opinion of you make or break your day.
26. Relax and reward yourself for a job well done.
27. Do things you love to do as much as possible.
28. Love your friends, family, and enemies alike.
29. Cut out the crap and timewasters.
30. Live by the 10,000 Hour Rule.
31. Spend thirty to sixty minutes alone thinking each day.
32. Design a life, not a career.
33. Introduce yourself as who you are, not what you do.
34. Embrace being a true self-starter.
35. Don't compare yourself to other people.
36. Stay on top of what's going on in your industry.
37. Associate only with positive, happy, and successful people.

A Very Valuable Skill

Reading is vital for leaders. By reading, we learn new skills that set us apart from people who don't read. The problem with reading is it's very slow and boring. Since it is slow and boring, people choose not to read. These people have never learned how to speed-read. Having the ability to read large amounts of information every day has made a dramatic difference in my life and the opportunities I can take advantage of.

When I first started educating myself, I read about a book a week. I would go to the library, pick up four books and return them a month later. My goal was to read thirty to forty pages a day. Eventually, I got down to reading a book in three or four days. Then two days. I really thought I was doing something. Now, I can read three or four books in a day.

Learning how to read faster is an essential tool for young leaders to develop. Many of the things you're going to need to learn are in written form. If it takes you six months to read five books and an hour or two to read through a few websites, you have a problem. Your solution is to improve your ability to read faster.

There are many different techniques and hundreds of different books and programs on how to read faster while still retaining comprehension. I've tried several methods. Some of them have helped, but in the end I had to figure out what worked best for me. Here's what works best for me.

The six things I do to read faster:

1. I eliminate all noises like the television, radio, or phone. Sometimes I wear earplugs.
2. I make the room as bright as possible so my eyes aren't strained.
3. I break the lines into two sections and scan from left to right.
4. I force myself to scan as quickly as I can.
5. I stop at important or good sections to read more thoroughly.
6. I take handwritten or copy-pasted notes to use later.

These techniques may or may not work for you. Try them. It takes practice. I spent hours refining my technique. You may not get it on your first try. There are many other strategies, faster ones, so find one that works for you. This one skill can make your self-education and personal development journey a much smoother and quicker process.

Speed-reading is a great tool to have, but I don't recommend using it for everything you read. I have found it's easier to speed through topics you're already familiar with and books or articles with a lot of meaningless filler. I don't recommend trying to speed-read through your math or law textbooks or any subject you're unfamiliar with.

A good area to begin practicing speed-reading is history. Try this exercise and see if it works for you — on a non-test or quiz day.

Based on class discussion for the next day, take fifteen to thirty minutes to speed read over the required reading chapters. If you have time left over, use the Internet to pull up a website or two about your topic and speed over those as well. When you get to class, gauge how much information you retained. You may surprise yourself at how much you remember.

You may find you want to kick yourself for not learning this skill much sooner. Think about all the time you spent hours reading stuff only to forget it the next day. Think about all of the time you blew off reading your material because you didn't want to spend the time on it.

Conclusion

There is so much to learn. As you continue the journey of personal development, you may need to try everything covered in this chapter and more, including strengthening your eye muscles, alternating your sleep cycles, and meditation. You will learn thousands of tips and techniques that set you apart from others. Have fun on your journey.

Visit www.cedericktardy.com to watch Video #4 titled *Speed Reading Exercises*. There are a few simple techniques and exercises to get you started with speed reading. If you're already a master at it, post your tips in the comments section below the video. If you have further questions, don't be afraid to ask.

Are you ready for your next action challenge?

Action Challenge

Action challenge number four is going to be one of the most enjoyable things you've done in a long time. I want you to take one to two hours (or more) developing your Lifelong To-Do List. Be as crazy, wild, funny, and unique as you possibly can with this. If you want to ride on the fin of a whale, put it down. If you want to base-jump from a skyscraper, put it down. If you want to donate $1,000,000 to your favorite charity, put it down. [All things on my list]

A good starting point for your list is, "How would I spend my year if I had a billion dollars to blow?"

The only catch? You need to come up with some sort of plan or strategy and timeline for how and when you want to accomplish everything on your list.

That last step is what sets people who accomplish their lifelong goals apart from those who don't.

Chapter Five: Job or Joy?

"Never continue in a job you don't enjoy. If you're happy in what you're doing, you'll like yourself, you'll have inner peace. And if you have that, along with physical health, you'll have more success than you could possibly have imagined." — **Roger Caras, president of ASCPA**

The late Roger Caras was a veteran of World War II, an author, and a television personality. His words set the tone for chapter five. It's important to recap a few of the lessons from chapters one through four before we dive into chapter five.

In chapter one, we discussed the Dream Team Concept. You learned to see your mother as the coach and yourself as the star player. In chapter two, I introduced you to the lifestyle of a young leader. This lifestyle consists of self-education, family, income generation, freedom, happiness, and some level of service for the good of the world. Then, we rolled into chapter three that focused on the education options for young leaders. You learned ways to excel in high school and college, the alternatives available to you, as well as the process of educating yourself.

In chapter four, you found a plan to fully embrace the personal development journey. You learned about the theory behind why some people succeed and others fail as well as the 10,000 Hour Rule.

Now, in chapter five, you'll tackle income generation. Income generation may be a new term for you, but it means how you make money. You don't have to live to work but instead can work to live. The difference is all in how you design your life.

People are going to give you a lot of advice about careers, jobs, schools, and what to do with your life as an adult. Many are going to advise you to get good grades, get into the best colleges, get scholarships, take out student loans, and graduate with the highest GPA you can. They're going to tell you that joining a fraternity and being active in school are important for your future. They're going to give you all sorts of advice. You've probably heard it all before.

Well, they're absolutely correct. If you want to get a good job, follow their advice. If you want to go to work for a Fortune 500 company and move up the ranks, follow that advice. Companies are looking for college graduates who understand the drive and dedication it takes to succeed in corporate America. Very few college graduates possess that inner drive.

But... What if you're like me and the millions of other people in the world who would rather poke themselves in the eyeball with a hot butter knife than put on a suit and tie every day and join the ranks of corporate America? Where is our advice?

This chapter is for those who may want to work for big companies but also for those who want to find an alternative.

What Is a Career, First of All?

A career is an occupation that requires a high level of training to fulfill and usually becomes a long-term primary focus in someone's life. Lawyers, doctors, engineers, professors, and astronauts are examples of careers.

So what is a job? A job is a position at a company that a person gets paid to fulfill based on hours worked and assigned duties completed. These positions may require some level of training, but the next person in the unemployment line could just as easily do the job. Examples of jobs include fry cook, administrative assistant, sales representative, or assistant manager.

Careers and jobs were created for two reasons: to further a company's objectives through hired work and to provide income for the working man and woman.

Young leaders understand there's a third option available. This third option is not taught in the classroom, and you don't prepare for it with textbooks. This third option is income generation.

Income generation is a term that describes creating money from means other than an occupation or job. Of the three options, income generation is the oldest form of earning money for yourself and your family. It wasn't until the First and Second Industrial Revolutions (roughly from the mid-1800s to the early 1900s when Western society became more mechanized) that people began to focus on getting jobs rather than pursuing entrepreneurship or farming. Examples of income generators include musicians, investors, businesspeople, freelancers, online marketers, and actors.

Whichever route you choose, young leaders understand that lifestyle design and happiness, not just money, are the goals. You can make money, a lot more money than you can at a job, doing a lot of things. Cocaine drug lords make a lot of money. Scam artists, too. Even hit men are paid well. If money was the supreme motivation for working, why wouldn't we all choose one of these options?

Myths Behind the Job

There are three myths that lead many people to make decisions about their future that, in the end, they're not happy with.

Myth #1: Careers are safer and more realistic.
When you discuss entrepreneurship today, people act as if you're asking them to complete a daredevil's final stunt and leap over forty burning cars rigged with explosives. In their eyes, entrepreneurship is risky, and getting a job or working in a career is the safest way to survive.

Truth: The truth is that more than 13,000,000 Americans are unemployed in 2012 according to the Bureau of Labor Statistics. A recent Gallup poll says that nearly one out of every four working Americans is underemployed, which means they're not doing work that makes the most use of their skills or pays them what they're worth. Not to mention that nearly sixty percent of 2011 college graduates have yet to find a job [in 2012], according to a recent article from CNN News.

Others will tell you that somewhere between fifty and ninety percent of startup businesses will fail within five years. People see this statistic and get scared. The truth is that whether you choose to work for a company or pursue your own sources of income generation, there are risks. It's up to you to decide what's more

64

important for your lifestyle design. Many people are preconditioned to think that money comes from a job, so they don't consider the other options.

Myth #2: Income generators do not offer benefits.

One reason to join a company is the extra benefits the company can provide. These benefits include things like vacation, paid sick days, medical insurance, and 401(k) retirement plans. Uninformed people believe they can only get these benefits if they work for someone else.

Truth: The truth is you can purchase medical insurance, take vacations, automate your income to provide for you when you're sick, and plan for retirement on your own. Check out SEP-IRAs, Single 401(k)s, or Easy IRAs for self-employment retirement planning. Visit www.ehealthinsurance.com to look at rates for individual, family, business, dental, vision, and other health insurance plans.

Get an idea of how easy this stuff is to set up on your own so you can make decisions for your future based on facts and not myths. And if you want to take a vacation, take one. While on vacation in Costa Rica, I met a man who had been on vacation for two months. His construction company built schools in Virginia. I asked him how long he planned to stay in the country. He said, "I don't really know." We continued talking on the beach as he fished with no bait on his hook—just happy to be free.

Myth #3: Either option is easier.

The last myth that many people have about careers or income generation is that either option is easier than the other. Some people say it's easier to get up and go to work every day to collect a paycheck. Others will tell you that finding your passion and purpose and creating a way to make money from it is easier.

Truth: The truth is that neither is easier. Each option has its difficulties. Whether you're fighting for a raise, time off, or just to keep your job or whether you're struggling to find new clients, create a new service, or sell an investment, you'll have difficulties.

There's no easy ride in anything you choose to do. If you find something that's "easy," jump ship as soon as possible. The old adage is true: "If it looks too good to be true, it probably is."

These myths have kept people in the dark for far too long. It's time for young leaders to think differently. This current economic situation is changing the face of the world, not just the country. We must look ahead to see what opportunities there are not just after graduation, but ten and fifty years from now when we have children and grandchildren of our own.

Generating Income for Young Leaders

Chapter eight takes you into the opportunities that are available. Here, we dive deeper into careers with innovative approaches to getting one and options available for young leaders. Also, there are listed several income generation options for young leaders today.

Careers

When looking for a career, there are basic things you need to do. You've probably heard this advice before:

- Make sure you're qualified
- Research the company
- Tailor your resume for the company
- Network with influential people inside the company
- Prepare for your interview

These five things are essential, but there are some innovative new approaches to landing that perfect job that young leaders are using today:

1. **Facebook Ads:** Take a minute to research Vanessa Terrell at www.vanessaterrell.com to see how she has used Facebook ads to generate leads for finding a job. Her approach is simple, inexpensive, and more effective than sending out tons of resumes.

2. **YouTube Interviews:** Create a digital interview and post it to YouTube. You can create a video of yourself and why you're qualified for a position. Or you can create a video presentation

demonstrating a project you developed and show the world just how talented you are. Google Feross Aboukhadijeh's YouTube interview and related media to get an idea of how this worked for him. He also created YouTube Instant Video.

3. **Direct Emailing:** Direct emailing is not a preferred method, but it's definitely effective at getting attention in a crowded marketplace. Start by researching companies you'd like to work for, like Google, for example. Go to the company webpage and look for a link that reads Jobs, Employment, Careers, Work for Us, or something similar. Read through all the information about the hiring practices, etc. You're looking for people with titles such as Hiring Manager, Recruiter, Staffing, etc. Search their names in Google to pull up their LinkedIn, Facebook, Twitter, or personal Web pages. For instance, I searched Google, learned Todd Carlisle was the Director of Staffing, and quickly found his LinkedIn profile.

There are so many options from here. You can email him directly through LinkedIn. You could join his Twitter. You can also contact the members within his list of contacts on the right side of the Web page.

Finding the person or people to contact is easy with the Internet. What to say to them that everyone else hasn't already said is difficult. I recommend starting a conversation with the people you're trying to connect with instead of bombing them with your resumes and desperate pleas for a job. Flatter them. Make them feel special. When the person responds, send him your YouTube video. You want to contact as many people as possible (more than fifty) from multiple employers (ten to fifteen), and contact each person once or twice a week for a minimum of eight weeks. If you don't get a conversation going after eight weeks, move on.

These are just three of the most innovative ways young people are finding jobs in a crowded marketplace. Gas costs too much to drive from place to place filling out applications, and that's an ineffective strategy anyway. Using these three approaches, you can also reach out to companies around the world.

There are different career options available to young people that may interest you as well. Two of them are startup companies and working abroad. A startup company is a newly formed business that's in search of talented workers with fresh ideas to get their enterprise moving quickly. These companies like to hire college graduates both for their energy and because they often work for a lower salary than an MBA with fifteen years of experience. Startups have their risks. Many startup companies fail and have to lay off their employees. This is a risk you accept because you believe in the company and its mission.

The term *working abroad* means to find work overseas. You can choose to join an international company in the United States that has offices in another country. Or you can choose to move to another country and find work as you travel. The most popular positions are English teachers, tour guides, American sales reps, and American business consultants, but there are thousands of other options.

Regardless of which career route you choose, you need to have three skills to succeed:

Skill #1: Ambition
> You need determination to succeed every single day you show up to work. If you walk through the front doors of your workplace with anything less than a mastery mindset, you're going to find yourself stuck in the same position forever or looking for another job.

Skill #2: Networking
> The ability to network or make connections that support your goals and dreams is essential for career success. Everyone should know your name at the company, and you should develop a reputation for dedication, loyalty, and hard work. Smile at everyone, introduce yourself to all, and attend every company social event.

Skill #3: Know the job

In order to excel in your career, you have to know your job inside and out. This means staying up to date on what's going on in your field. For some occupations that may mean reading industry news and reports every morning. In other careers, you may need to get recertified every year. Whatever the requirements are, fulfill them on time and to the highest standard possible. However, you need to take this a step further. It's also a good idea to know your job two levels up and one level down. This means to understand what your boss does, what his boss does, and what the people underneath you do. By understanding all these positions, you become the go-to-guy for the company, and that's how you make yourself more valuable.

Income Generators

If a career isn't a part of your lifestyle design, consider generating income instead. There are many benefits to avoiding the career wheel. For example, when you learn to create money on your own, you can never become unemployed. Also, you have unlimited income potential because you're no longer working by the hour or for a salary. Finally, you have the freedom to work when, where, and how you want to as long as your customers and clients accept the way you choose to work, or it fits into a workable business model.

Here's a list of eight income-generating options available for you today. These are by no means the only options. Read through these options to get ideas and inspiration.

1. **Freelancer:** A freelancer is someone who works for a company without any long-term agreements. They offer services such as accounting, graphic design, writing, sales, consulting, legal advice, campaign strategies, etc. They can make no money, little money, lots of money, or millions.

2. **SME:** SME stands for small to medium enterprise. Small business owners operate a company that has one or more people working for it. These businesses can operate in any field from cosmetic development, pet grooming, to software design, and everything in between.

3. **Artists:** Artists range from musical to graphic and everywhere in between. Artists can become celebrities or write the music or storylines behind the scenes. They can create logos for businesses or decorate hotels and corporate offices.

4. **Fitness coaches:** Personal trainers typically work at a gym. Fitness coaches work for themselves. They travel to people's homes, hold their own events, or sell products to their customers to generate income.

5. **Investors:** Investors can invest in stocks, real estate, options, currency, or businesses. It takes money to get started.

6. **Internet marketing:** Internet marketing is a broad term to describe making money online through selling products, selling ad space on your website, selling services, flipping domain names, etc. There are thousands of options within Internet marketing or online businesses.

7. **Professional athlete:** Professional athletes are not confined to the NBA, MLB, NFL, or NHL. You could choose to pursue car racing (there are many kinds), boxing, MMA, PBR, PGA, the Olympics (money comes from the endorsements, not the Olympics themselves), fishing, beach and regular volleyball, etc. There are a ton of options both in the United States and overseas.

8. **Inventor:** An inventor is someone who creates a new process, product, or service and sells it for income to companies or governments that use it. One thing people don't know is that you don't have to come up with something unique. You can simply improve on existing ideas and develop a patent around that improved product.

Weighing Your Options

When weighing your options for a career, a job, or an income generator, you always want to remember that you're planning *your* life. This is not your counselor's life, your parent's life, or even your girlfriend's life. It's yours. Consider the education requirements, location opportunities, benefits offered, ambition required, lifestyle promised, and the legacy you'll leave behind when making your decision.

Think long-term. Think about whether the choice you're making brings you closer to where you want to be in life or not. If the answer is no, don't walk down that path. You won't be happy.

Another important point to keep in mind is that your income generation decision today doesn't have to be your final decision. In the past, you studied for a specific career, and you worked in that field until you retired. Today, you can choose to switch from one field to the next every year if you want. Don't feel as if you have to limit yourself because everyone else recommends doing so.

Redefining Success

Redefining what success means to you is how you can truly develop the lifestyle design that best fits your personality. If you let Warren Buffet define success for you, you need to live in the same home you grew up in, create a billion dollar investment company, pore over technical investment data daily, and work until you older than seventy. If you let Richard Branson define success for you, you need to break world records and run 300 companies. If you let Jay-Z define success for you, you need to sell millions of CDs and marry Beyoncé.

There's nothing wrong with anything these men have done. But is what they do the same as what you are best suited to do? Are you any good at rapping? Would you know what to do with a billion dollars if I told you to manage it for fifty years? Could you even think through how you would manage 300 companies? Even if you worked with one every day, you would barely get to them all in a year if you worked every single day.

For most people, success is measured by *money*. The amount of money someone has in his wallet, bank account, around his neck, on his wrist, in his garage, and for some, on his teeth shows the world he's succeeded. Beamers, Benzes, and Bentleys are the goal for some. Private jets, fifty-room mansions, and models on their arms symbolize success for others.

But what's important for you?

Young leaders in America are starting to realize that a Prius can get you to the same place a Porsche can, and the money saved can be put to better use. These young people no longer define success as cars, clothes, women, and money. They measure success in fun, freedom, happiness, and the ability to do what they want, when they want, and how they want.

Consider these five examples of men who have redefined success as income, impact, influence, and insane fun.

Tim Ferriss has received many awards, including being named *Forbes* magazine's "Names You Need to Know in 2011." He's the author of the book that started a revolution in America, *The 4 Hour Workweek*, and an angel investor for companies like Facebook, Twitter, StumbleUpOn, and Digg. Ferriss has led an extremely astonishing life that includes traveling the world, running profitable online automated businesses, National Chinese kickboxing champion, and Guinness World Record holder in tango. On top of all of this, he's an education reform promoter who has built several schools overseas.

Cullen Jones is the third African-American swimmer to make the Olympics. His journey started when he was five. He nearly drowned on a water ride at an amusement park. This incident forced his mother to sign him up for swimming lessons. A few years later, Jones earned a gold medal as a member of the U.S. 400-meter Freestyle Relay team. He now uses his fame and fortune to encourage minorities to learn how to swim working with the USA Swimming Foundation's Make a Splash program.

Mark Ecko is the creator of the billion dollar Ecko fashion line. He's not only a fashion designer but also an entrepreneur, investor, artist, and philanthropist. In his teenage years, he built a design studio in his parents' garage where he began creating and marketing T-shirts, customizing hip-hop clothing, and airbrushing girls' fingernails. His business exploded, and his clothing is now worn around the world by people of all races. Ecko founded a nonprofit, Sweat Equity Education, to increase the success of urban, underserved students. He also has launched multiple social activism campaigns including Stop Dissing Me, which seeks to introduce students' voices to the education debate.

Lupe Fiasco is a rapper. He started creating music in his father's basement as a teenager and eventually made it big. His message goes beyond the drug dealing, killing, and obsession with money you hear in so much rap music. "I want to start a popular uprising," Fiasco says on the Summerfest website. "The music is the bait to get people to come in and listen to what I'm saying." That uprising is based within a manifesto around the acronym LASERS, which stands for Love Always Shines Every time: Remember to Smile. In this manifesto he says, "We want substance in the place of popularity.... We will not compromise who we are to be accepted by the crowd." Fiasco uses his fame to raise money for several organizations such as Summit to Summit and the Music for Relief charity.

Jordan Romero is a teenage mountain climber who made world headlines by becoming the youngest person to climb the world's seven tallest mountains. At age ten, Romero climbed Mt. Kilimanjaro in Africa, and at age thirteen, he climbed Mt. Everest in Asia, the world's highest mountain, at 29,035 feet. He has even written a book titled *The Boy Who Conquered Everest: The Jordan Romero Story*. He travels the country speaking to young people. His message is clear, "You can do anything."

These people decided to do what they wanted to do. They each chose to design their lifestyles around something they loved and used that love to create income. There are millions of examples of people who realize that money doesn't have to come from a job. Instead, they think about lifestyle, income generation, and happiness.

The Dream Team and Your Career or Income Generator

Your ability to communicate your career or income-generating ideas to your mother effectively may determine whether or not you can follow your dreams. Each of the people above had families who were heavily involved in their pursuits. Imagine what Mark Ecko's father thought when his son told him he wanted to make hip-hop clothing and airbrush women's nails. Imagine what Lupe Fiasco's parents thought when he decided to make music a fulltime career? How did these men get their parents to believe in them enough to not only allow them to follow their dreams but also to support them along the way?

Simple.

They started by realizing that their parents would most likely disagree with their choice of "work." The disagreement came from traditional thinking clashing with newer thinking. Rather than get upset, these young men understood the different perspectives. By having open, honest, and well-thought-out conversations, they helped their parents to see how confident and competent they were. They explained the real reasons why they wanted to go against the traditional and recommended lifestyles. Most important, they involved their parents in their dreams.

When you're ready to discuss your income generation ideas with your mother, follow their lead. I had these same conversations with my mother before I launched my first books and started my nonprofit organization. I showed her how confident I was and invited her to get involved in what I was doing.

There are tons of ways for you to make money in life. If you look, there are hundreds of ways for you to make money now. You can create an account on Fiverr.com and begin using your talents, social media following, or skills to generate income today. This may not be the income generator that buys you a fifty-room mansion, but it could generate enough income to allow you to purchase a home study course and the equipment you need to start the business you want.

Conclusion

There's so much to learn about career and income generation. I hope this chapter has inspired you to think further ahead and deeper than you have before. The next chapter focuses on learning about money and investing. After all, you have to know what to do with your income once you get it, right?

Here are three excellent books to help you along the way.

The first book is *Rich Dad Poor Dad: What the Rich Teach Their Kids about Money — That the Poor and Middle Class Do Not!* by Robert Kiyosaki. This book was the first book I ever read on personal finance and income generation. I have never been broke since.

The second book is *The 4 Hour Workweek: Escape 9-5, Live Anywhere, and Join the New Rich* by Timothy Ferriss. This book helped me understand there was an even better way to live than I already was living. I learned the concept of automating my business.

The third book is *I Will Teach You to Be Rich* by Ramit Sethi. This book taught me about the four pillars of personal finance — banking, saving, budgeting, and investing, as well as the ideas of personal entrepreneurship.

I have read more than 100 other books on the subject as well as taken some really intense home study courses, but these three books are must-reads if you plan to escape the rat race, as Robert Kiyosaki would say.

Remember: You can do anything. You can climb mountains or win Chinese kickboxing championships. You can pursue as many different dreams as you want. Or you can choose to enter a career field and excel through the ranks of corporate America. Whichever route you choose, do your research, understand your options and obstacles, and then go for it.

On my website www.cedericktardy.com, you will find Video #5 titled *Using the Internet to Make Money Today*. In this video, you learn step by step how you can start making some money on the Internet today. That video could be worth thousands of dollars to you.

Action Challenge

To complete this action challenge, you need to create a list of career or income generation ideas. This list needs to have at least twenty ideas. Create this list with your mother. Under each item on your list, develop a good reason why it's a great fit for you.

For example: Become a commercial diver. This is a good fit for me because I love to dive and travel. The entry into the field is fairly low cost, and the salary is decent if you're qualified for certain jobs.

Chapter Six: Collecting Paper?

"In this country, first you get the money, then the power, then the woman." — **Tony Montana aka Scarface (from the movie *Scarface* starring Al Pacino)**

Disclaimer: The financial advice in this chapter is solely my opinion. It's based on research as well as personal experience. You can choose to follow all, some, or none of this advice.

I believe the entire movement of glorifying cocaine and crack-selling to get rich needs to stop. I quote Tony Montana from the movie *Scarface* not because I believe in his methods for getting rich but in his philosophy about money. I believe Tony had it right when he told Manny exactly how this country works. I think young leaders can and should rephrase it, however, to read, "In this country, first you generate income, then use it to have an impact, and then you start a family."

This chapter's not about collecting paper. Collecting money alone is a fool's game. Instead I am going to teach you as much about money as I can in one chapter. Understanding what money is and how it works is critical to your family's survival, your lifestyle design, and the degree of impact you can have on the world.

Why Am I Qualified?

You may be wondering whether I'm even qualified to teach you about money. After all, I'm not a multibillionaire. Why should you listen?

In my defense, I'm a finance major. I have read more than fifty books on investing alone plus another fifty or so on personal finance. I have some real war stories in both investing and financial management that have given me enough experience for you to learn at least a thing or two. I have a credit score that fluctuates between 760 and 816 and always has since I was eighteen years old. But in the end—like most people—I'm not extremely rich.

If I could tell you one thing that would give you confidence in me, it's this: This chapter is not about getting rich. It's about the basics that all young leaders need to understand to keep from being poor.

Getting Into Money Thinking

The difference between people with some money and people with no money is all in the mind. For example, I end my years differently from most people I know. Rather than try to budget in Christmas gifts I can't afford, I start estimating my next year's income. I subtract all of my expected expenses from the total. I do this because it gives me an idea of what my spending limits are. I do this because I respect the value of a dollar and the influence each dollar has over my lifestyle.

It works like this. Let's say my income generator (in this case, the Army) was paying me $65,000 a year. I subtract the yearly total of my bills from my expected $65,000. I subtract $12,000 for my mortgage payments, $8,400 for taxes, $1,200 for my cell phone, etc. By the end of all of the subtracting, I have around $37,000. I then subtract how much I want to save that year. Let's say my goal is $20,000. This leaves me with $17,000. I then need to subtract my estimated expenses on food, gas, clothes, and other things I need to survive. This may bring my total down to $8,000.

In my head, I would know I have $8,000 to spend for the year on traveling, hobbies, additional education, emergency expenses, etc. Most people never take the time to think their money all the way through. Their credit reports show this. I didn't always think like this. It wasn't until I understood money from the ground up, the basics, that I became financially responsible.

Money From the Ground Up

There's a lot to learn about money. Throughout my studies and experience, I realized there are eight things everyone should understand about money and how it works.

1. Money is a means of trade that's socially agreed upon. By itself, the cotton fiber paper mixture we know as the dollar is worthless. If you had a time machine and could go back 500 hundred years with a million to spend, you'd see just how

worthless it is. That society wouldn't recognize the value it holds. When you understand that money is worthless and that the social agreement about money is where its value and power lies, you get a better idea of how to make more of it.

2. The U.S. dollar is one of the world's dominant currencies. It holds this rank along with the euro, the pound, the yen, the Canadian dollar, and the franc. Of these, the British pound is the most expensive currency at the time of this book's printing.

3. The U.S. Bureau of Engraving prints U.S. dollars, and the Federal Reserve manages the amount of money in the system.

4. The value of the dollar goes up and down all day long based on economic factors and speculation.

5. The overall value of your dollar goes down year by year due to inflation. The *time value of money* says that money available at the present time is worth more than the same amount in the future.

6. Banks are a secure place to hold your money when you're not using it. Banks play an important role in the financial system by controlling interest rates, offering loans, and providing other services to businesses and people. But banks are not your friends; they're businesses out to make money, too.

7. There are trillions upon trillions upon trillions of dollars in the world. No one really knows how much wealth there is in the world. This wealth is not held in cash. The majority of the wealth in the world is in real estate, business values, stocks, natural resource reserves, etc.

8. Money is only made in one way — by exchanging a product or service, otherwise known as sales. Whether you're raising money for an organization, working at the local grocery store, selling books to families, or developing cures that eradicate diseases, you're selling a service, a product, an idea, a dream, or a hope.

Money Myths

There are ten money myths I believe everyone must realize are lies. Continuing to live by these lies will only hold you back.

Myth #1: Money is the root of all evil.

This myth comes from a misquoted scripture in the Bible, 1 Timothy 6:10, which says, "For the love of money is a root of all kinds of evil. Some people, eager for money, have wandered from the faith and pierced themselves with many sorrows."

Truth: This scripture is not saying that making money will harm you. Continue to read the entire passage, and you find the Bible encourages the rich to use their wealth generously to do good deeds for the good of humanity. If having money made you evil, the Bible would tell you to give all of your money away and never make another dollar. But it doesn't. It says to use your wealth, wealth that you have generated, to make a positive impact on the world.

Myth #2: You can make a lot of money selling drugs.

If you believe the movies and music, you might think you can make a lot of money selling drugs on the street.

Truth: The truth is that pharmaceutical companies like Johnson & Johnson, Pfizer, and Merck are making money selling drugs. All the people on the corners are hardly making enough to get by. The average street hustler makes little more than minimum wage. The drug lords and cartels are making some money, but at what costs?

Myth #3: If I work and save for forty-five years, I can retire with wealth.

Most so-called financially intelligent Americans believe that if they work hard every day for forty-five years, save ten percent or more of their income, invest it wisely, and wait until age sixty-six or older to draw it out, they will have enough to live on for the rest of their lives.

Truth: The truth is, the math doesn't add up, even when you add in investing. The average American makes $45,000 to $55,000 a year.

Let's assume you're lucky enough to make $70,000 a year for your entire forty-five-year working life. This would total $3,150,000 of total earned income. When you begin subtracting things like mortgages, cars, food, gas, health expenses, vacations, kids, education, etc. from the number you realize you won't have even $1,000,000 left. And you need more than $1,000,000 to live unless you plan on spending the last years of your life eating hotdogs and Top Ramen.

Financial advisors will tell you that investing your money in a mutual fund or stock will help you to earn five to ten percent interest a year on your savings. The truth is that hardly anyone will earn a return of ten percent a year on their investments, especially during volatile times. This retiring generation has seen its investment accounts wiped out due to violent market fluctuations. And even if you gained five percent a year and somehow managed to save $2,000,000, by the time you're sixty-six or older, you could easily use all or most of it on medical bills if you became ill even with Medicare.

Myth #4: A six-figure job is the epitome of success.
Some people believe that if they can earn $100,000 or more a year, they'll be okay. After all, it's far more than the average of $45,000.

Truth: The truth is that as your income goes up, so does your standard of living. As you earn more money, you buy bigger and more expensive toys. This reduces your savings potential. Even if you saved all of your $100,000 a year for forty-five years, it would only equal $4,500,000, which is about what you would need to retire comfortably — today.

Myth #5: I need to save ten percent of my income.
The financial advice at the turn of the 20th century was to save ten percent of everything you make and never spend it. If you invested it wisely, you would wind up a multimillionaire. This advice was sound — for the turn of the century. I used to follow this advice. Then I bumped my savings target to thirty percent of my income.

Truth: The truth is, saving ten percent of your income is better than not saving at all, but you should do your best to save more if at all possible. Most people spend more than ten percent of their monthly income on their cars. If you're going to start building wealth, try to save twenty-five to fifty percent of your income into different savings categories.

Myth #6: I need to have millions of dollars in the bank to retire.
Most Americans have a number in their heads of how much money they need to retire. They develop a plan with their financial advisors and then work every day to meet the plan. These people are considered financially intelligent. Once they reach their goal of $2,000,000 or more, they stop working and live their dreams.

Truth: The truth is that having a target amount in the bank to decide when you can retire is not enough. A couple in their sixties could potentially blow through $2,000,000 in less than twenty years when you think about medical expenses. Many Americans are living past the age of eight-five these days. Do you want to try to die before you run out of money, or would you rather live comfortably and have money to leave your family? The key is not a certain amount in the bank but instead passive income. Passive income is money you make effortlessly from investments and good planning.

Myth #7: I need to work until I reach retirement age.
The United States has set the retirement age at 66 now, and it will go up to 67. People in the work force believe they have to work until that age until they can retire. Imagine working from fifteen or eighteen all the way until sixty-seven. Fifty-two years or so of working with two weeks of vacation a year equals a total of two years of vacation time.

Truth: The truth is you don't have to work until whatever age the government says you are allowed to retire at. You only need to work until you reach financial freedom. Financial freedom means enough money in the bank to be comfortable, enough passive income to live on, and no debt.

Myth #8: A financial advisor will help me to get rich.

Most people don't know how to manage their money. Rather than learn on their own, they choose to hire a financial advisor. They believe this person's years of experience will help them to get rich.

Truth: The truth is that financial advisors work for banks or investment firms or are brokers who sell products designed to make money for themselves as well as the companies. If you happen to make some money from the products, the businesses are happy too because then they can charge you more fees. Financial advisors are salespeople. They make commissions on what services they sell, not necessarily on how much money they make you.

Myth #9: I can't afford that.

The motto of the poor is, "I can't afford that." Ask them why they don't buy a book series that could help them, they say, "I can't afford that." Ask them why they're not taking extra college classes, and their reply is, "I can't afford that." Ask them why they've never taken a vacation. They will tell you, "I can't afford that."

Truth: The truth is that if you continue to tell yourself you can't afford something, you never will. Everyone, rich or poor, has things that are just out of their current reach financially. Some people make plans to earn and save the money to get what they need, and others make excuses.

Myth #10: I'm too young to worry about money, investing, credit, insurance, business, etc.

As I travel the country, I listen to young people's excuses for why they're not worried about gaining financial intelligence. The overwhelming excuse is age. They believe they can worry about "bills and stuff" later.

Truth: The truth is they're right. They can worry about bills and stuff later but at what cost to their lifestyle design. Every successful young leader you've met in this book started his or her first enterprise, for profit or not for profit, with money they saved from working, birthdays, and Christmas gifts.

Your Lifestyle Design and Your Financial Plan

Your lifestyle design and your financial plan must be in line. If not, you'll find yourself in debt with a failing enterprise. In order for your design and plan to line up, you must become financially intelligent. The eight topics you must be wise on are:

1. **Making money:** Making money comes from selling goods and services. There are millions of ways to make money. Find the ones that work for you. Create multiple streams of income. I recommend at least ten.

2. **Saving:** You should save for different purposes. Each purpose should have its own bank account (i.e., retirement, investment, education, vacation, down payment, etc.). Understand the time value of money and how it affects your savings.

3. **Investing:** Know all the different types of investments available to you such as American Depository Receipts (ADR), **angel investing**, **common stock**, **annuities**, closed-end investment funds, collectibles, convertible securities, corporate bonds, futures contracts, life insurance, money markets, mortgage-backed securities, municipal bonds, **mutual funds**, options, **preferred stocks**, **real estate**, real estate investment trusts (REITs), treasuries, unit investment trusts (UITs), and zero-coupon securities. I have **bolded** the ones that interest me. Your focus with any investment is ROI (return on investment).

4. **Taxes:** Taxes are fees the government levies on products, services, and income. These fees are used to support the government and many of the programs that help you. Study up on tax law. Taxes are your largest expenditure.

5. **Giving:** Most wealthy countries, businesses, and individuals are givers. Whether you believe in karma or not, giving can result in a big tax write-off for you. As you look to grow and protect wealth, learn how to give it away wisely.

6. **Credit:** Credit covers everything from credit cards to credit scores and everything in between. Mismanagement of your credit can affect your chances of landing a job or getting funding for your enterprise.

7. **Budgeting:** Budgeting is important. Learning how to think ahead with your finances allows you to make plans for your family vacations, your education, or new investments. You eventually need to use budgeting software, but for now just focus on spending less than you make.

8. **Asset Ownership:** Assets are things you own that either increase in value as they age or produce income on their own. In short, assets make you money. Rich people buy assets. Poor people buy stuff.

Unless you're already a financial genius, you're going to want to learn more about each one of these areas. Remember the tips from chapter three on self-education and make use of the Internet to start increasing your financial education over the next weekend. Start with one of these subjects and read a few articles. Your entire lifestyle design depends on your financial IQ. It's not selfish to learn about money. It's wise.

Your Dream Team and Its Financial Plan

Your family's Dream Team Concept will rely heavily on the family's financial IQ. Families rarely discuss the idea of building a financial plan, which is why many are broke and in debt. Too many households in this country are living by monthly payments. Have a serious discussion with your mom about the family's financial plan.

Topics you want to discuss are: total yearly income, total yearly expenses, total amount currently in savings, the total amount of debt, total value of assets, how much money you need per month as a family to live out your dream, alternative income generators, plans to increase income and savings, and plans to reduce debt and expenses.

These conversations can make or break your household. If your family is in bad financial shape, get serious about fixing the problems. Visit the Department of Labor website at www.dol.gov and research programs your family may qualify for. Your mother may be too busy or too stressed out to do this on her own. Show her what you've learned and ask her for other ways you can help.

Remember there are other options besides getting a job to bring in extra income. Even if you found work for $10 per hour for forty hours a week, you'd only bring in around $350 a week after taxes. While this may be better than nothing, if you don't fix the bigger budgeting problems, your extra income and time will be wasted. Build a plan. Focus on other income generators available to you. In short, get involved.

If after having the financial talk with your mother you find out you aren't in any financial trouble at all, don't sit back with your feet kicked up and laugh at the rest of the world. Use your good fortune to help others by volunteering. Learn the skills you need to manage the wealth your family has. Avoid becoming another spoiled and reckless American teenager. You can even research investment opportunities your family is unfamiliar with and bring them to a discussion.

My Journey With Money

Regardless of your current financial situation, realize that your Dream Team and your lifestyle design rely heavily on your ability to make good financial decisions.

My household was not poor, but we weren't rich, either. We went through our fair share of financial troubles, and they motivated me to want to make more money. I was the type of kid who always had some business going on around the neighborhood or apartment complex. I can remember starting a lemonade stand, a trash removal venture, and a lawn mowing business. I would wash your car wash, pressure wash your house, or walk your dogs. In high school, I tried to make faster money by selling weed, pills, and other stuff.

Eventually, I smartened up. I learned how to manage money by watching people. I noticed that people with money behaved differently from people without money. Eager to learn more, I started reading books on the subject, and soon finance became my passion. I opened my first investment account at eighteen.

I started day trading shortly after and did okay at it for what I understood about the market. I majored in finance in college. When I was twenty-two, I got out of the Navy and started my first legitimate business, Cederick Tardy Enterprises. It went okay for a little while, but there was a lot I didn't know about growing a business. In time my passion moved into real estate, and I bought rental property.

Always wanting to continue expanding, I re-formed Cederick Tardy Enterprises, and this time made it a LLC (limited liability company). The S.T.R.O.N.G. Association began to grow as well as I began to learn more about business and money. Today, I have several different income generators. Each one of them allows me to live the life I designed for myself, support my family when they need it, and give back to others.

Everyone needs money to survive — even the homeless. Learning how to wisely manage the money you earn can be the difference between living to work and working to live. Mismanagement of finances is one of the leading causes of depression, suicide, family splits, and divorce. When finances are aligned, the freedom you have allows you to focus on things that matter, and you can enjoy life.

There are thousands of books on the subjects of personal finance and investing, but these four are good starts.

The first book is *Rich Dad Poor Dad*. I mentioned this book already in chapter five. It's a must read. The second book is *The Millionaire Next Door* by Thomas J. Stanley. I recommend reading *Losing My Virginity* by Richard Branson. Finally, I recommend reading *Succeeding Against the Odds* by John H. Johnson. These four books are completely different from one another, and so together they provide a well-rounded view on financial education and personal finance.

As you continue your financial education, I recommend reading a lot of biographies and "how I did it" stories from successful millionaires and billionaires. These people have actually made it to financial success. Many authors who write personal finance books, real estate books, and other business books make their money from selling those books and speaking, not from the advice in their books. Learn from people who know.

Last, I recommend only taking financial advice that helps you achieve your lifestyle design plan — even if that means throwing out all of the advice from this chapter. You have to do what is going to work for you. So even if you throw out all my financial advice, make use of that one sliver of wisdom, and you'll be happy.

There are hundreds of websites on finance. Here are five websites to start learning about finance and investing. Use the pointers from chapter three to guide you.

1. Investopedia.com
2. Mymoney.gov
3. Bankrate.com
4. Khanacademy.org
5. Smartmoney.com

Conclusion

Hopefully this chapter has encouraged you to learn more about money and how to manage it wisely. The more you understand, the more opportunities you can see. Remember that money is cotton fiber and paper with ink on it. Alone it has no value, but because society has decided you will eat, commute, and educate yourself based on the amount of money you have, it is important.

Don't forget to watch Video #6 titled *How to Build a Dream Team Financial Plan* at www.cedericktardy.com. In this video there are the tools and techniques you need to lead your family in the right financial direction.

Your next action challenge awaits you.

Action Challenge

For this action challenge you will be figuring out what your Dream Team's income goal is for a month. To do this, you need to think about all the components your team says are important for your dream lifestyle. Estimate how much you think it costs a year to live that lifestyle.

Take that number and divide it by twelve. That is the amount of money you need to focus on generating every month. You can divide that number by thirty. This gives you the daily income goal you need to meet in order to live the lifestyle you dream of.

Don't worry about how big the number is. Focus instead on what you can do to generate that amount of income. Next, focus on how much money it will take to create the income generator you will need. Then, think through how you can earn those startup funds.

The point of this exercise is to get you to think past getting a job to earn money.

I was introduced to this story awhile back. You may have read it before. In case you haven't, enjoy.

The Story About a Mexican Fisherman

A businessman was at the pier of a small coastal Mexican village when a small boat with just one fisherman docked. Inside the small boat were several large yellow fin tuna. The businessman complimented the Mexican on the quality of his fish and asked how long it took to catch them. The Mexican man replied, "Only a little while."

The businessman asked why he didn't stay out longer to catch more fish. The Mexican said he had enough to support his family's needs. The businessman then asked, "What do you do with the rest of your time?" The fisherman replied, "I sleep late, fish a little, play with my children, take a siesta with my wife, stroll into the village each evening where I sip wine and play guitar with my amigos. I have a full and busy life, señor."

The businessman scoffed, "I'm a Harvard MBA, and I could help you. You should spend more time fishing and with the proceeds buy a bigger boat. With the proceeds from the bigger boat, you could buy several boats; eventually you'd have a fleet of fishing boats. Instead of selling your catch to a middleman, you could sell directly to the processor and eventually open your own cannery. You'd control the product, processing, and distribution. You'd eventually need to leave this fishing village and move to Mexico City, then Los Angeles, and eventually New York City where you could run your expanding enterprise."

The fisherman asked, "Señor, how long will this all take?" The businessman replied, "Fifteen to twenty years." The fisherman replied, "What then, señor?" The businessman laughed and said, "That's the best part! When the time is right, you'd announce an IPO, sell your company stock to the public, and become very rich. You'd make millions." "Millions, señor? Then what?" said the fisherman.

The businessman said, "Then, you would retire. Move to a small coastal fishing village where you would sleep late, fish a little, play with your kids, take a siesta with your wife, stroll to the village in the evenings where you could sip wine and play your guitar with your amigos."

The fisherman, still smiling, looked up and said, "Isn't that what I'm doing now?"

Chapter Seven: Women, Sex, and Scandal

"Man does not control his own fate. The women in his life do that for him." — **Groucho Marx, comedian and film star**

Disclaimer: Some of the tips in this chapter can be misused to take advantage of people. That is not the intent. Use the information in this chapter for good only.

The power women have over our lives is immeasurable. They're our mothers and grandmothers. Most of our schoolteachers are women. Women fill most of the healthcare positions in the country. This chapter is about women, how they influence our lives, and the issues men tend to have with them. This chapter covers relationships, dating, sex, virginity, what women want from men, how to spot a good woman, love, and so much more.

This subject is going to be extremely important for you as you grow into a young leader. Men who lack an understanding of the things you're about to learn lead unfulfilled, lonely lives. Some even ruin their reputations playing by the wrong rules. It's time for you to start seeing women for who they truly are.

Women and Their Challenges

There are several myths about women. The world has so many views on who women are, why they exist, and even where they came from. To this day there are still women with no civil rights, living in slavery. These myths here barely touch every issue concerning women, but these four are the most important for young leaders today.

Myth #1: Women are dumb.
> We've all seen the hot girl who can hardly spit out a sentence without acting like a shy toddler. We've all seen women who can't drive. We've all seen women who completely forget what they're saying as they talk. Many men have come to believe that all women are this ditzy.

Truth: The truth is a large percentage of women are exceptionally intelligent and well-educated. The majority of women are so much smarter than most guys they pretend to be less intelligent so they don't make the men around them insecure.

Myth #2: Women are weaker.

Women's bodies are built differently from yours and mine. Men's bodies were created for heavy lifting and smashing things. Women's were designed for having and raising children. Because of this, their bones and muscles are smaller than men's on average. Some men believe that because men are physically stronger than women, they can and should control them.

Truth: The truth is that not all women are physically weaker. I've seen women in the military outperform men in running, pull-ups, grappling, pushups, sit-ups, and rope climbing. Even many civilian women are much more physically fit and physically stronger than many men. Take a moment to Google "women's power lifting" and read the story of Angela Cavallo, the mother who lifted a Chevy Impala off of her trapped son.

Myth #3: Women cannot control their emotions.

When women get upset, scream, cry, or act "unladylike," men are quick to think or say, "It must be that time of the month." When men discuss the idea of a woman president, they joke about how World War III or a nuclear war could be the result of one bad conversation during that time of the month. Joking or not, these thoughts influence the way we see women.

Truth: The truth is that while PMS can have a dramatic impact on some women's moods, many times you'll never know when a woman is on her cycle. Most women don't complain, act out, or do anything irrational even though they may be in significant pain. Both men and women have temper issues. Men shut down, fight, yell, punch or kick things, or try to drink their problems away. Women may cry, yell, shut down, fight, hit things, or try to drink away their problems as well.

Myth #4: Women are only good for cooking, cleaning, sex, and raising children.

This is old world thinking. Nevertheless, some men still think this way. They treat women poorly and talk down to them simply because they're women.

Truth: The truth is that women have fulfilled every role from being a mother to serving in some of the highest positions in companies like Meg Whitman at eBay and in government (as of this printing, the current Secretary of State is a woman, and her two predecessors were women). Yet around the world, women are still forced into slavery for sex and labor. Read the stories of Moulkheir Mint Yarba of Mauritania and the horrors of sex trafficking taking place globally.

In America, women who stand up for themselves and push back against the injustices are called bitches, dykes, sluts, and even Rush Limbaugh's favorite, femi-Nazis. In the 21st century, women still face discrimination in churches. The Catholic and Orthodox churches and many conservative Protestant denominations still only allow men to be ordained as clergy. Women have to navigate a double-bind. When they assert themselves powerfully, people perceive them as not acting feminine enough. When they act in the stereotypically feminine way, they aren't seen as strong enough to be leaders.

Even if you believe all these myths are false, you must understand there are still millions of men who have little to no respect for women. And this isn't just about women you'll never meet. This is your mother, your sister, your grandmother, your aunts, cousins, and nieces. This is about your girlfriend(s) and your future wife. Every day, they face a battle for equal treatment.

According to the National Center for Injury Prevention and Control, more than 13,000 women are abused every day in this country. According to a National Crime Victimization Survey, more than 600 women are sexually assaulted every day in this country.

Have you ever seen or heard men talk about abusing women mentally, physically, sexually, or emotionally? Psychologists say that abusive men are possessive, controlling, insecure, manipulative, and abnormally sensitive. These traits go against everything a young leader stands for.

Ten Great Women

Young leaders should value women and their contributions to society. Consider the impact these ten women have had on the world:

Oprah Winfrey
Oprah Winfrey is the one of the most influential woman alive. She's most famous for her television show, which was the highest-rated program of its kind in history. Winfrey is a multibillionaire and has appeared on every list you can name that ranks influential people. On top of the immense influence she had on multiple generations of women and men in America, her organizations The Angel Network and the South African Leadership Academy for Girls have changed millions of lives.

Mother Teresa
Mother Teresa founded the Missionaries of Charity in Calcutta, India, in 1950. At the time of her death in 1997, the charity operated 610 missions in 123 countries helping people in need. For more than forty-five years, Mother Teresa ministered to the poor, sick, orphaned, and dying. She earned numerous awards, including the Nobel Peace Prize.

Eleanor Roosevelt
Eleanor Roosevelt was the First Lady to the late President Franklin D. Roosevelt. She fought for human rights and was part of the supporting members who formed the United Nations. During her time at the United Nations, she chaired the committee that drafted and approved the Universal Declaration of Human Rights. A bronze statue of Roosevelt stands in the southern end of New York's Riverside Park at the corner of 72nd Street and Riverside Drive.

J.K. Rowling
J.K. Rowling, a single mom, was a poor British novelist. In the late 1990s, she released the *Harry Potter* book series and proceeded to sell more than 400 million copies. The *Harry Potter* series became the

greatest selling series of all time and made J.K. Rowling extremely wealthy. Rowling established the Volant Charitable Trust, which combats poverty and social inequality and gives to organizations that aid children, single parent families, and multiple sclerosis research. She has many more charitable notations.

Mary Kay Ash

Mary Kay Ash is the founder of the Mary Kay Cosmetics line. She started Mary Kay with a $5,000 investment, and before she died in 2001 the company had more than 800,000 representatives in thirty-seven countries, with total annual sales of more than $2 billion. She received numerous awards for her business' phenomenal growth and impact on the lives of women around the world. The Mary Kay Foundation is still in operation supporting organizations that fight cancer and violence against women.

Benazir Bhutto

Benazir Bhutto was the 11th prime minister of Pakistan and to this day the only woman to have ever held that title. She fought for economic growth, national security, and human rights in Pakistan although she was relentlessly criticized. She was assassinated by bombing. A year later, she was awarded the United Nations Prize in the Field of Human Rights. Her influence in government in a Muslim region known for its deplorable treatment of women will forever be remembered.

Angelina Jolie

Angelina Jolie is one of the highest paid actresses. She has won several awards. While she may be most famous for her role as Lara Croft, Jolie promotes humanitarian causes and is noted for her work with refugees as a Special Envoy and former Goodwill Ambassador for the United Nations High Commissioner for Refugees. She served as a Goodwill Ambassador for over a decade and used her fame to establish several charitable organizations. She is known worldwide for being beautiful, brilliant, and benevolent.

Alyssa Milano

Alyssa Milano is another actress who uses her fame to make an impact in the world. Milano was appointed Founding Ambassador for the Global Network for Neglected Tropical Diseases. The Global Network is an alliance formed to advocate and mobilize resources in the fight to control neglected tropical diseases. Milano is a UNICEF Goodwill Ambassador for the United States. She has raised tens of thousands of dollars to support several organizations around the world fighting against AIDS and diseases and advocating for animal rights.

Selena Gomez
Selena Gomez is an actress and singer best known for her role in the Disney Channel television series *Wizards of Waverly Place*. Her music albums have gone platinum, and her songs have reached number one on the *Billboard* charts. When not making headlines for acting, music, or her relationship with Justin Bieber, Gomez is actively involved in the world. She has been involved in the UR Votes Count campaign, St. Jude's Children's Hospital *Runway for Life* benefit, and RAISE Hope for Congo. She became the youngest UNICEF Ambassador ever at seventeen. This is on top of starting a fashion line and so much more.

Women are out doing some amazing things, gentlemen. These are just ten women who have made and still are making a huge impact in the world. This list fails to cover women's influence on breakthroughs in medicine, psychology, government, space, business, technology, etc. We are going to need to step our game up. Big time.

The Man of the Year

Each year *Time* magazine creates a list of the Man of the Year (now Person of the Year). This is an honor bestowed upon such great people as Charles Lindbergh, Gandhi, President Dwight Eisenhower, John F. Kennedy, Martin Luther King Jr., and Mark Zuckerberg for their influence on the world. As young leaders, we should strive to meet the level of distinction needed to receive such an award. Imagine being named Man of the Year. Outside of doing something extremely phenomenal, part of this award is about the character of the man.

The definition of a *gentleman* has changed a lot throughout history. Originally, this was a title reserved for the rich. I believe it's important for young leaders today to understand what a gentleman is.

A gentleman is someone who is educated. He takes care of his family. A gentleman is not a copycat. He is unique, courteous, and refined. One of the best character traits of a gentleman is that he lives and dies by a code of honor. His word is his bond. Men can trust his handshake.

These are some of the high standards a gentleman lives by. He:
- Remains polite and courteous — the better man
- Is bound by his word
- Tries his best not to curse
- Avoids speaking loudly to keep from raising the stress level in others
- Keeps his cool at all times
- Doesn't interrupt others
- Respects his elders
- Doesn't laugh at others' mistakes
- Waits until everyone is seated before eating
- Helps a woman companion with her seat
- Offers help to a lady in need
- Always opens doors for others
- Offers to give up his seat to women, the sick, or the elderly
- Never grooms himself in public
- Is always on time
- Shakes hands firmly with strong eye contact
- Doesn't kiss and tell
- Genuinely thanks others for their help
- Pays the bill (It's ungentlemanly to argue about who will pay the tab)
- Engages people around him in conversation
- Never speaks with food in his mouth
- Walks on the traffic side of a sidewalk
- Respects his mother and women in his family

These rules don't restrict a man; they make a man. While it may not seem like the coolest code of honor, as you get older you'll see that high-level women are crazy about men who understand what it means to be a gentleman. Low-level women? They're actually repelled by a man who lives by a code of honor. Two birds, one stone.

What Women Look For in a Man

While I can't speak for every woman on the planet and I don't claim to, I can tell you the women I know generally are looking for these six traits in a man:

1. **Intelligence:** Use your intelligence to surprise an attractive woman with off-the-wall fun ideas, fantasies, and unexpected things, and she will find it hard not to find you attractive.

2. **Uniqueness:** Stand out from the 1,000 other guys who hit on her all day long by being different. The number one thing you can do to be different is be a young leader.

3. **Be generous:** Amaze women by showing them you spend your time thinking about the welfare of others. Make a donation, help out someone less fortunate, donate time at a soup kitchen, or volunteer at a shelter. Invite her along to see you in action. This will impress her. And by the way (and much more importantly), you'll be doing good for the world, too.

4. **Focus:** Women love men who know what they want and go after it. Set a goal and then go after it with passion.

5. **Sense of humor:** Slight overconfidence combined with an awesome sense of humor works. Women appreciate a genuinely funny guy who flirts a little, shows them a good time, and then still has a full life of his own.

6. **Leadership abilities:** Many women are attracted to men who have men following them or trying to be like them. Many women love men who can inspire others to action. Many women love men who are in charge.

Dating

Understanding the dating game early is important for your development as a young leader, in my opinion. As a young man, eventually, if it hasn't happened for you already, you'll become obsessed with the idea of women, dating, and sex. These three things will consume a majority of your waking thoughts. Failing to understand dating, relationships, and sex now will only amplify their significance in your mind.

Men who can't get a date spend their days searching for women and their nights doing the same. Men who can get a date spend their days focused on their passions and their nights with the woman of their dreams. For this reason, I feel it is important to help you put the subjects of women, dating, and sex into perspective.

What is dating? Dating is simply connecting with women who share similar interests with you and enjoy time with you. Dating has nothing to do with sex, long-term relationships, commitment, mind games, or any of that. Dating is about finding connections with women, building friendships, and ultimately learning more about yourself and others.

There are many myths about dating. The biggest is, "Nice guys finish last." If you believe this myth, you probably think women love bad boys and find nice guys boring. In order to get a woman, you will think you need to act big, bad, tough dangerous, and basically like a dick.

The truth is that women do tend to be more attracted to bad boys than nice guys, but the term *nice guy* needs to be properly defined. When most people think nice guy, they are really referring to shy soft tempered guys. Being a gentlemen and being a nice guy are two different things. Most men don't realize this. They think being a gentleman will keep them from attracting women.

Gentlemen don't finish last; *men without self-confidence do.* Men who lack the confidence to ask a woman out or express the way they feel about the girl they like will always be kept in the shadow of the confident and cocky guy out making girls smile and laugh.

Men have probably used pickup lines to get a woman's attention since the dawn of time. Three examples of pickup lines are:

1. "What does it feel like to be the most beautiful girl in this room?"
2. "Fat penguin" (She says, "What?") "I just wanted to say something that would break the ice."

3. "It's not my fault I fell in love. You're the one who tripped me!"

Relying on cheesy stuff like this to attract a woman is not a good idea. Rather than using pickup lines and hoping they work, keep these *must-know* dating tips in mind when entering the dating world. *Please only use these tips for good!*

Master flirting: Women have great instincts and can easily detect when someone is not sincerely interested. Successful flirting only works when there's a mutual attraction. Flirting involves being confident, playful, fun, and mysterious. Use all the tools of body language like eye contact, smiling, being attentive, playing, touching, etc., and combine them together to show that you really are interested in her.

Do not chase: The problem with some men is they think that in order to get a woman they must constantly give women attention. Wrong! The reason some women get bored in a relationship, or turned off, is that they get too much attention.

Show interest: Ask her questions about her life, favorite music, movies, or foods, her goals, and opinion on current events. Say things that make her laugh, but avoid being offensive. Avoid jokes about socially uncomfortable subjects.

Reveal some things about yourself: Discuss your dreams or goals for the future and talk about how you plan to achieve them. Many women hope to find a man who's ambitious, and they're willing to play a supporting or partnering role. It may help if you treat the lady as a potential teammate.

Be yourself: Above all, the most important thing to know is be yourself. Don't try to wear sunglasses, hats, jackets, chains, Hollister, or talk differently if that isn't who you are. There are more than seven billion people in the world. The most important one is you. Show her that you respect yourself and are proud of who you are.

Once you master the tips of attracting a woman, you can use these three tips to land a date:

1. Be confident in your request, regardless of whether the answer is "yes" or "no."
2. Start with a small request like going to get food after school or lunch on the weekend. The first time you ask her out should not be for prom.
3. Just say it already. The worst thing she can do is say no. You weren't dating her before. You'll be just fine.

If you're following the lessons in this book and becoming the young leader you know you can be, you'll get the date — trust me. Use these four tips to build an impressive date:

1. **Creative versus expensive:** Your date doesn't have to cost a lot. It needs to be fun and imaginative. Is there a festival in town? Is there a free yoga event at the city park? Is a big celebrity signing autographs at the mall? Do some research beyond looking up a movie's time.

2. **Plan everything ahead of time:** You should have your date planned. Meet on time and know exactly where you're going. You should never ask, "What do you want to do?" Know exactly what there is to do in and around your city and bring the ideas up as if they're just random thoughts. Bring all the things you need such as beach towels, blankets, food, mountain climbing equipment, or whatever.

3. **Line up multiple events:** Have after-date plans already in mind to keep the good day going. For example, you two decide to go tubing at the lake or have lunch at a cafe. Is there a concert later that night? Bring it up while you're tubing or eating lunch. Invite her to go with you. If you're having fun, she'll go. Have dinner plans for after that.

4. **Provide opportunity for conversation**: The most important component of dating is talking. Your outing should provide things to talk and laugh about. Going to the movies can be part of your day, but it should not be the entire date because you have no chance to talk. Examples of places that allow you to

talk and laugh are the mall, a festival, a volunteer day, or the beach.

When you're dating at this level, you'll pull far ahead of the other guys. Use these skills wisely. No mind games. No using people. Dating is about fun. As this fun develops, it will mature to kissing.

Have you ever seen a romantic movie where the guy goes for the kiss? There are birds, music, and dancers. As the scene climaxes, he sweeps the woman off her feet and gets the girl. Well, that rarely happens in real life. There probably won't be doves, and the director won't cue the music for you. It is up to you to make the moment special.

You can help make the kiss special by not rushing. Create anticipation. Make her want to kiss you. When you two finally lock lips, relax. Keep your eyes closed. And have fresh breath!

Everyone kisses differently. You learn from person to person. Tongue, no tongue, touch face or not, hug or not, bite lips (gently) or not, etc. It all depends on the one you're with. Eventually, you develop things you like and things you don't like. Be honest with yourself and with your partner.

Sometimes, things go awry.

Things may start out well, but there may come a time when the relationship no longer works for the two of you. That's when you break up. Rarely do you marry the first girl you ever dated, so it's important to understand how to handle a break up without ruining your reputation and getting caught up in a lot of unnecessary drama.

When the relationship is going downhill, it's so easy to end it. There's no need to drag it out. Sit her down and end each other's pain. She'll understand where you're coming from. Tell her exactly why you're breaking up. Tell her she's a wonderful, amazing woman, but you can't give her what she needs.

She may get angry, and she may say any number of things, but she'll respect you for handling the break up maturely. Don't get into arguments with her afterwards or some sort of competition to find another person first. No drama.

If she breaks up with you, don't get angry. Handle it maturely. Don't argue, plead, cajole, denigrate. No drama.

Keeping dating in perspective is important. Understanding how to handle the entire process should help you prioritize dating. Dating should rank above watching television or playing videos games, but below creating your lifestyle design and your Dream Team.

Finally, you find someone special and enter into a "serious relationship." Use these four tips along the way:

1. Date many times doing different things.
   If you want to turn a casual relationship into a serious one, don't think of sex as a top priority. Focus more on things that build the relationship, like talking, planning, and enjoying experiences together. Be patient; establish a strong bond, and the rest will fall into place.

2. Don't rush it.
   Don't feel as if you have to display your newfound love right away. No need to rush out and buy a ring or post your love for the girl all over the Internet. At the beginning of a relationship, it's all about taking things slowly.

3. Act romantically.
   From time to time, surprise her with a candlelight dinner, flowers, or something special. Let her know you do, in fact, have a romantic side. You may not want to do this every day. Spread these moments out so they're special.

4. Honesty is the best policy.
   Live by a code of honesty. Telling lies or covering things up about yourself will only lead to problems later on.

The Perfect Woman

There are billions of women in the world. How do you know who's right for you? Keep these qualities in mind as you're dating. You'll see your Miss Universe when she appears. Here are qualities to look for:

- She's independent
- She's intelligent
- She's beautiful inside and out
- She respects you
- She understands that men and women are different and allows you to be yourself
- She gets along with your friends and family
- She loves you for who you are and doesn't try to change you
- She makes you want to be a better man

Women you want to avoid have these character traits:
- Liar
- Gold digger
- Ungrateful
- Disrespectful
- Unreliable
- Stingy
- Slutty

Let's Talk About Sex

Sex is such a big part of our lives. It's a shame that more adults don't feel comfortable talking about it with young people. Failing to understand sex and its role in life can harm a young man. The mystery will cause him to spend many years lusting, experimenting, and trying to find something that isn't real.

Pornography and the media use sex to sell things and make money. The sex industry makes more than $20 billion a year. Church and school programs tell you the exact opposite of what the media does. We end up exposed to a lot of myths, lies, and confusion. Because of the way our country treats the topic of sex, it has made sex into something it isn't.

What Is Sex?

Sex is simply the process of inserting a man's penis into a women's vagina. That's it. Other ways to have sex acts are anally or orally. Sex is not pornography. Sex is the way we produce babies.

Sex is an essential part of life. Nature created us to reproduce. We have instincts that drive us to want to reproduce. Testosterone, a steroid hormone the body produces naturally, makes you a man. It helps you through puberty. It's the driving force behind your sex drive.

I believe understanding sex from this point of view takes the mystery out of it. When you were a little boy, you never worried about sex. Then, all of a sudden, it was the only thing you could think of. Why? Why does it seem like every other thought in your mind is about sex?

The answer has a lot to do with testosterone and your growing instinctive urge to have sex. This is completely natural and normal. No one should ever tell you differently. You should never feel guilty about your increased urge to have sex.

Sex is bigger than just an instinctive need to reproduce, though. Sex is a way that humans bond with each other. The act of having sex is usually pleasurable for the people involved. Through having sex, people develop a closer bond with one another.

Sex also has many health benefits. Researchers have shown that having *protected* sex regularly with your partner can reduce stress, anxiety, improve mood swings, and reduce the risk of some cancers. Not to mention the entire activity is a workout for the muscles and lungs.

Sex Has a Dark Side

Sex is complicated in a social sense. The first issue to know is that some people use sex to deal with their emotional pain and distress. They have sex with people in the same way a drug addict uses chemicals: to cover up the pain. This is important for you to understand for two reasons. One, you should take care not to attach yourself to women who seek sex to deal with their emotional problems. These women don't need sex—they need help. Be a bigger man and talk to these ladies. Explain to them that you see what they're trying to do. Let them know there is a better way to deal with their problems. And if you really care, get them some help.

Some men take advantage of these insecure, unhappy women. They use them for sex, and throw them away; the cruel ones turn them into prostitutes. Young leaders shouldn't fall into the same trap. Would you want someone to treat your mother, sister, or daughter this way? How about your grandmother? Think about it.

The second thing to understand is that you also can easily become the type of person who uses sex to cover pain. This is a losing game. There's nothing good on the other side of the short orgasm. Though it may feel good for the moment, many people who live this life will tell you it never turns out well. The pain remains. Get real help.

Sexually Transmitted Diseases (STDs)

Another villain that terrorizes the dark side of the sex world is the STD. STDs are a *huge* risk that counters any possible health benefits sex brings. Consider these facts before you jump in the sack:

- There are more than 25 different types of sexually transmitted diseases. The most common are: chlamydia, gonorrhea, syphilis, genital herpes, human papillomavirus (HPV), hepatitis B, trichomoniasis, and bacterial vaginosis.

- The Centers for Disease Control estimates there are 19 million newly acquired STD cases in the U.S. each year. STDs are so common that more than half of sexually active adults will acquire an STD at some point in their lives.

- STDs like chlamydia, gonorrhea, herpes, syphilis, HPV, and HIV/AIDS are transmitted through vaginal, anal, or oral intercourse. Infections are passed along even in the complete absence of symptoms. Only regular STD testing, coupled with protection during sexual activity, can limit the risk.

- The World Health Organization estimates there are at least 340 million new cases of sexually transmitted diseases every year among people ages fifteen to forty-nine.

I don't tell you these facts to scare you. I want you to be aware. You have to know what is really going on. Wearing a condom is better than not wearing one, but they can break. Also, herpes can be passed through skin contact around the condom. Consider yourself warned and choose your partners carefully.

Unplanned Pregnancy

Unplanned pregnancies can lead to a real departure from your lifestyle design because babies change everything. I once heard a comedian joke about KIDS being just as scary as AIDS. As funny as the joke was, the truth is pretty serious.

Creating another human being like yourself is not something to take lightly. Whether you have a long-term relationship with the mother or not, you still bear responsibility for the child, financially and emotionally. Think cautiously before you leap and remember birth control is better than nothing, but it can fail. Are you ready for kids? Are they part of your lifestyle design? Are you ready to discuss morning-after pills and abortion? Abortion, whether you believe in pro-choice or not, is taking the life of a human being. That is a heavy burden.

Sex Questions We All Have

If you're older than seven, you've probably had many different questions about sex. The truth is that most men have the same questions. Many don't find the answers they're seeking for a long time because no one is brave enough to answer their questions. Below I have done my best to answer four of the top questions we have all had about sex:

Is my penis big enough?

This question bothers men for most of their lives. You hear people bragging about nine inches, ten inches, even having a penis that drags on the floor! Studies have shown that an average length is between 4.5 and 6 inches. If yours is bigger, brag to your friends if you want. Just understand that size isn't the only thing important to women. Women's opinions vary greatly on the issue of size, but they all agree knowing how to use it is most important.

How do I have sex?

If you haven't had sex yet, wait. I know you don't want to get to college or even later and be inexperienced, but wait. The truth is the more sex you have, the less you care. You end up being bad in bed anyway. Tips to great sex are:

1. Have sex with someone you care about and who cares about you.
2. Take your time. You're not a rabbit.
3. Treat your partner with respect. Ignore just about everything you saw in porn or heard in music.
4. Have conversations about what you both like and dislike.
5. Practice with the one you're with.

When should I start having sex?

This depends on your family's rules, your religious beliefs, and your decisions. There are legal considerations to keep in mind, also. The age of consent ranges from fourteen in Arkansas to as old as eighteen in California. Know your state's laws before engaging in sex with anyone under the age of 18. Check IDs. Based on personal experience I recommend waiting to have sex, even if you have already started. Focus on getting your life together. Women will come, trust me. However, the older you get and still lack direction, financial stability, and personal character, the less women will find you attractive.

Is it okay to masturbate?

Some religions tell you that masturbation and sex are sins. Ask them to tell you what you're supposed to do with the millions upon millions of sperm your body produces every day if you can't have sex or masturbate. Research has proven that masturbation helps men improve their immune system, reduce the risk of prostate infection, and reduce the risk of prostate cancer. Relieve yourself, but don't let masturbation and pornography consume your entire life.

Virginity

Being a virgin is not a curse. Society will tell you that boys who have not had sex are socially incompetent. You may start to believe you're not a man until you have sex. None of this is the case. If you have these doubts, the first thing you need to do is relax. Don't put so much pressure on yourself. The person who falls in love with you is going to respect you. If you're worried about premature ejaculation due to inexperience, don't be. It happens to everyone. You can read up on the subject. A helpful tip is to masturbate four to eight hours prior to having sex.

Girls can be very sexually aggressive. They may tease you about being a virgin. That's okay, too. While they're teasing you, there's another girl, a good girl, watching you to see how you behave. Will you follow the crowd or be true to yourself?

Protection
Wearing a condom is the smartest decision you can make when you become sexually active. They're uncomfortable and can get expensive, but so can STDs and kids. I recommend using them every time. Even with the same woman. You just don't know whether she's faithful, and you may have more than one partner. Ludacris, the rap artist, is such a believer in condoms he became the Trojan Man. He's the face of Trojan's Magnum condoms.

Here are two websites that currently offer free condoms. You may need to pay around $6 for shipping and handling, but it's worth it.

www.clubcondom.com
www.condomusa.com/4free.asp

In addition to these websites, many nonprofit health organizations, schools, and universities offer free condoms to promote safe sex. Check with your nurse's office or counselors. Do not be embarrassed.

Conclusion
You just got a crash course on women, dating, and sex. Use the info wisely. Remember that as young leaders, you should treat women as you want someone to treat your mother, sister, or daughter.

Don't let women and sex go to your head. You hear about famous men in the news all the time who have let their poor decisions about women and sex damage their name. Men such as Kobe Bryant, Bill Clinton,

Tiger Woods, John Edwards, and most recently the Secret Service members in Colombia have all fallen into this trap.

Go out and become the "Man of the Year." not the "news story of the week." Visit www.cedericktardy.com to watch Video #7 titled *Planning a Good Date*. This video has some helpful tips for planning a good date.

Action Challenge

Your challenge is to create three questions to ask women, either in person or on your social media website of choice. The purpose of this challenge is to get you to see that asking intelligent questions is a better way to get women to talk to you than pickup lines.

Example questions:

Current Event Question: "How do you feel about the way the Secret Service agents are being treated after the prostitution scandal thing made the news?"

Social Opinion Question: "Why do you think some men think women are stupid?"

Casual and Silly Question: "If you had one wish from a genie, what would you ask for?"

Chapter Eight: Social, Political, Economic, and Environmental Issues

"I began to see the future not as a totally impenetrable realm about which we can know absolutely nothing, but rather as an exciting frontier, offering enormous possibilities but also extraordinary dangers. We cannot possibly know everything that lies ahead, but with effort we can glimpse the possibilities of our future. This weak but incredibly valuable knowledge is critically important if we are to make wise decisions." — **Edward Cornish, Founder of the World Future Society**

The ending for this book changed several times. I didn't know how to wrap up a book that has taken you through family empowerment, lifestyle design, personal development, self-edification, career advancement, financial education, and relationship advice. What more could I possibly give you on top of the videos, on top of the personalized comments, on top of the action challenges? Then it struck me. I had not given you the understanding of the world that a young leader must have in order to find his place in the big picture.

Chapter eight is about gaining an appreciation for the global issues. There are a lot of things that are messed up. It's time for young leaders like us to look at the future in a new way. While many Americans are thirsty for more of life's riches, there are billions of people who are still just thirsty. They have no clean water to drink.

Living in America, you may think that someone else's problems halfway around the world don't affect you, but they do. It's even scarier to think problems like lack of food, dismal education, and an inability to find work are American issues, too. People in your city, your state, and your country are in need of your help.

Many people hear talk like this and immediately stop listening. They don't believe people should receive handouts. They don't believe in welfare. They don't believe in free healthcare. They believe in all sorts of myths about doing something good for humanity.

You must understand the world's issues go far beyond charity and nonprofit organizations. They're going to take young leaders like you to create profitable companies, ideas, and strategies to fix the mess out there. This is your introduction to a bigger world. Get involved in whatever way you can, as a volunteer or an entrepreneur.

Abundance

I'm not sure how familiar you are with the news, but if you've watched at least one news show in the past ten years, you know the world economy is in trouble. There's so much negativity out there. That is why I was so surprised to see a book released in 2012 titled *Abundance*. The authors Peter Diamandis and Steve Kotler did an amazing job of introducing regular people to advances in technology and thinking that are positioned to have a large impact on the way the world operates.

In this book, three forces are presented that the authors believe will play a dramatic role in improving the world. Understanding these three forces and how they impact the world can give you ideas of what the future has in store.

The first is the influence of the few billion poorest people in the world who have recently begun plugging into the world economy, both as consumers and as producers of goods as a result of the communications revolution. Internet-capable devices are cheaper than ever and give people around the world a voice. Imagine billions of new minds able to communicate with the rest of the world for the first time instantaneously through YouTube and Facebook. What new ideas and possibilities are out there?

The second influence the authors introduce is the impact the new breed of wealthy individuals is having on privately funded technology projects. The "techno-philanthropists" are giving more money than ever to efforts that attempt to create global solutions to issues such as energy, food, health, and water shortages. Imagine solving the issue of turning saltwater to freshwater economically. You could form a trillion dollar company.

The final focus of the book is on the rising phenomenon of small organizations and even individuals who are making worthwhile contributions in the most advanced technological domains such as computing, biotechnology, and space travel.

Before I read this book, I was involved in several organizations in my community and donated to charities around the globe. After reading it and launching into my own self-study program on the issues at hand, I gained an even wider view of what people like us can do to make a profound difference. It all starts with understanding how much the world has already changed.

The Last Twenty Years

When I was in elementary school in the 1990s, things like Wi-Fi, iPhones, Google, social media, video blogging, and apps didn't exist. The Internet started to become a big deal when I was in junior high, and everyone had to have it so they could instant message on AOL. We still used phonebooks and walked around with change in our pockets to make phone calls at payphones. Cell phones were only for rich businessmen. If you got lost while driving, you had to pull over and ask for directions or purchase a map at a gas station.

I'm 27 at the time of writing this book. Now, my iPhone allows me to shoot high-def videos with excellent audio and upload them directly to my YouTube channel, which then allows me to edit them and add effects before posting my videos to my Facebook and Google+ pages, blog, website, and email marketing campaigns. All this happens in the palm of my hand while sitting on my couch eating Sun Chips watching *30 Rock* on Hulu. With the swipe of my finger I can check my stocks, my business inventory, or the weather for tomorrow's fishing trip.

None of this was even a thought in the average person's mind just twenty years ago. Today, these are ordinary technologies. Many jobs are now erased due to the technological advances in logistics, sales, manufacturing, and research that have occurred in the past twenty years. At the same time, many new fields have been created. Degrees that were once valuable ten years ago are not even taught today. What do the next twenty years have in store? What's your outlook on the future?

The Three Outlooks

As I travel for business and pleasure, I like to talk openly about the issues we all face to gather opinions on the state of the world. I have found there are three general outlooks for the future:

Outlook #1: Passive
> These people accept and allow what happens and what others do around them without any response or input.

Outlook #2: Complacent
> These people are satisfied already. They have all they need and are either unaware of or don't care about the dangers, troubles, or opportunities that exist around them.

Outlook #3: Progressive
> These people are pushing the limits every day. They're advocating for and implementing new ideas and reform movements in all sorts of areas ranging from marine preservation to politics and technology.

The people in the last group are leading the world in some shape or form. They're creating the world we see. The other two groups are merely living in the world created around them. Those with an "I can create my future" attitude are creating successful businesses that solve global, national, and local issues.

America the Great

Most of us believe that America is the greatest country in the world. We're taught to be patriotic. We're taught to believe our country ranks at the top in education, commerce, healthcare, government, food supply, technology, and social behavior.

While I haven't traveled to every country on the map, I have visited enough and met people from even more places to see that our country is starting to really fall behind in every one of those areas (and others). As a whole, we have failed to learn and understand multiple languages or cultural differences from other prominent countries around the world. Many of us have never watched a movie produced in Bollywood, but in India there are millions who understand the English language better than you or I. And they can speak and understand several other languages, too.

The rest of the world gets it. We don't. This national attitude of passivity and complacency will continue to slow our country's growth in every global industry.

America's Issues

Regardless of whether we are quadrilingual as a whole or not, this is still one of the greatest countries that has or will ever exist, in my opinion. Nevertheless, we have some *huge* problems that young leaders desperately need to make a priority. If we ever want to stop worrying about jobs and the sagging economy, we're going to need to do something about the way we think. These are seven of our country's major issues where our new ideas can have the largest positive impact:

Issue #1: The national debt
>   Our country spends more money than it makes, and we are almost $15 trillion in debt. We need to focus on growth, not just budget cuts, to solve the problem.

Issue #2: Aging population
>   People in this country are living a lot longer than they used to, which puts an economic burden on their children and the government programs that provide for their retirement and care.

Issue #3: Job loss
>   Hundreds of thousands of jobs are disappearing every year due to advances in technology and outsourcing to countries with cheaper labor. At the same time, new jobs are created that most jobless people aren't qualified to fill.

Issue #4: Globalization
>   Every year, the world's economy grows more globally integrated. As this continues, more jobs shift from nationally based to having offices around the globe, causing more people in the U.S. to lose their jobs.

Issue #5: Trash
America produces 250 to 275 million tons of trash a year. That's five hundred and fifty billion pounds of trash. We recycle only about thirty-five percent of it. The rest goes into our landfills, oceans, or sidewalks.

Issue #6: Aging infrastructure
According to the American Society of Engineers, our country's airstrips, bridges, dams, levees, railroads, energy grids, highways, schools, and wastewater systems are in need of $2.2 trillion worth of upgrades and repairs to meet our economic needs. These issues are hurting our economy and chances to remain a superpower.

Issue #7: The education system
Educationally, we rank 14th in reading, 17th in science, and 25th in math out of the top thirty-four countries in the world.

These are just seven of the issues this country faces that are hurting the economy and affecting our future. As young leaders, we shouldn't worry or fear. Rather than see problems, we should look for and create amazing opportunities to have a massive impact and influence that can lead to mega income. From now on, when people tell you that your generation's problems are with gangs, drugs, alcohol, STDs, obesity, music, grades, or something else, remind them of these seven bigger troubles.

Even Larger Problems
If America has so many issues, you can only imagine how much trouble the rest of the world is in.

For starters, the world's population has risen to more than seven billion people and is expected to reach 10.5 billion by 2050 or sooner. Of these seven billion, almost eighty percent live on less than $10 a day, $3,650 a year, according to a World Bank report. This extreme poverty leads to malnutrition and disease-related deaths. UNICEF reports state that more than 22,000 children, young kids, die every single day (eight million a year) because they don't have medication, food, clean water, or energy to support life.

Another one billion children who make it to school age are not in school. These kids can't read or write their own names, let alone make a positive difference in their communities and the global economy. How are their countries ever going to come out of poverty at this rate?

All around the world, water, food, healthcare, education, and energy shortages coupled with slavery, senseless wars, and mass slaughter go on while we dream of another pair of shoes or flip channels on our high-definition televisions. In Mauritania, ten to twenty percent of the population is still enslaved. In Haiti, people still suffer from the massive earthquake of 2010 even though the news cameras have left.

As the population continues to grow, it's going to be more difficult to feed us all. Over-fishing has wiped out many of the edible fish species in the oceans, lakes, and rivers around the world. Over-farming has stripped the land of nutrients, forcing further deforestation in order to create more fertile farming areas. While food production has increased drastically since the revolution in agriculture, the technology that fuels the entire food supply relies heavily on oil. As oil prices increase, so will food prices.

Vast improvement is needed in all of these areas: climate change; global finances; food and agriculture; arms control; trade and economies; politics; the military; healthcare; human rights; terrorism; and conflict resolution. These are not someone else's problems. They're everyone's problems. A major war in the Middle East could drive up oil prices and cause worldwide inflation. A disease outbreak affecting fish, grain, livestock, or water would decimate the population.

It's important that young leaders realize these millions of people who are dying are more than statistics. They're human beings with friends, families, purposes, and passions. It's even more important that we don't get worried or scared by these issues. Within these problems lie potential for unlimited developments.

Solutions Already Taking Place
These global issues are not going unnoticed. Millions of people are making a difference every day. Education reform is taking place because of global programs like Universal Primary Education, a goal of

the United Nations Millennium Development. Energy reform is taking place in the exciting fields of nanotechnology, biotechnology, solar, and wind technologies. Computer science is continuously being revolutionized, and the technological results improve every issue we face.

Governmental reform is taking place globally, as well. Many countries are banding together to fight human rights injustices, terrorism, and corruption. Financial and economic movements are making a difference. Organizations such as the World Bank and Kiva, a micro-funding nonprofit organization, are helping to reduce global poverty. Advances in the military's use of UAVs, robotics, satellites, and strategic partnerships are reducing terrorism and civil wars around the world. Food production, water treatment, healthcare, natural resource management, and environmental health all have people and organizations doing great things for the good of us all.

People Making a Difference

While some choose to sit by and do nothing, others are taking action by seizing opportunities. In March 2012, Carlos Slim Helu, a Mexican businessman, was named the "Richest Man in the World" for the third time by *Forbes* magazine. Helu amassed his fortune by controlling more than 200 companies. He credits his success to his ability to spot opportunities for growth before other people.

Dean L. Kamen, an American entrepreneur and inventor, is trying to make a huge impact by solving the world's most alarming problem, the freshwater shortage. He created a piece of technology called the Slingshot. The Slingshot can transform polluted water, saltwater, or even raw sewage into incredibly high-quality drinking water for less than one cent per liter. It can produce enough water to serve a village. On top of this, it generates enough power to run itself and other equipment. This machine has changed lives and is leading the movement for clean water.

In government, Shirley Franklin made history and much needed improvements for the city of Atlanta. During her term as mayor (2002 to 2010), Franklin created several infrastructure projects to improve the city's economy. She created the Clean Water Atlanta Act to improve the city's aging sewage systems and repair old water pipes. This had a dramatic improvement on the city's chances of avoiding any future water shortages. Thirty-five states still need to make these improvements in their major cities.

In food production, Dickson Despommier, a microbiologist and ecologist at Columbia University, is leading the movement with ideas to create vertical farms. Vertical farms are ways to economically and environmentally cultivate plant or animal life within skyscrapers, or on vertically inclined surfaces. This idea would allow large quantities of food to be produced in a much smaller area than a regular farm, for instance, inside major cities, and reduce transportation costs. His designs would run on solar power.

In energy production, Tetsuji Yoshida of Japan introduced an idea that could solve the world's needs. After the nuclear disaster in Japan following the earthquake and tsunami in 2011, Yoshida's idea of a Lunar Ring began to gain popularity. The Lunar Ring would be a belt made of solar panels placed around the moon's equator that could power the Earth. Yoshida's idea would be the largest public infrastructure project in human history. It would produce 20 trillion watts of power a year, and would pay for itself in fifteen years.

Young people like Malal Diam Sow, Natsuno Shinagawa, and Ryan Hreljac are examples of what young leaders are doing to make a difference. You can read about them and their impact at www.unicef.org/people. These young people's ideas, including ideas like my books and nonprofit, were once just the idea of a single person.

Within each of the problem areas facing the world, our country, your state, your city, and even your neighborhood are hundreds, thousands, and millions of opportunities to use your ideas to create change and income. For example, as a civil engineer, you're looking at a $2.2 trillion industry in the coming years as America plans to rebuild its aging roads, waterways, and airports.

Young leaders, find your passion and get in the game now.

Planning Ahead

Your family's future is affected by all of these issues and hundreds more. Your mother's ability to maintain a job or run a business, your grandparents' ability to retire comfortably, as well as your future children's education and social experiences are all getting formed now by these global issues. Your entire lifestyle design is dependent upon energy, healthcare, technology, food, water, and logistics. Sadly, few people understand this the way you do now.

No one can predict what job markets or income generation fields will boom twenty years from now. Things that are working today or next year may not even exist in the next fifteen years. Nevertheless, there are six skills you need for sure, both now and in the future.

1. You need foresight to see changes coming and make wise decisions to help you, your family, and your plans avoid trouble or take advantage of opportunities.

2. You need the ability to think outside of the norm. The problems we have today aren't solved because the ideas needed to fix them don't exist yet.

3. You need the ability to operate in many cultural environments. Skills such as being multilingual and knowledgeable of other customs, governments, and economic systems will set you apart.

4. You need the ability to take lots of different ideas, information, and opportunities and communicate them in simple enough ways for others to understand the issue.

5. You need the ability to use all new forms of global communication technology.

6. You need the ability to understand concepts, ideas, and challenges in many different fields so you can piece them together for new solutions.

These six skills are essential. They take time to develop, so start now. The world needs people like us to stand out from the crowd. Overcome your family issues and your personal issues with the tips and techniques on building your Dream Team and a lifestyle design best suited for you.

The Last Stretch

Often, the one thing holding people back from making a life change is not knowing which direction to go. It's easy to get inspired to make a difference, but when you get ready to go out and do something... That's another story altogether. Below are six different directions to think about if you want to pursue a life of not only income, but impact. These options encompass lifestyle designs for you, your family, and your friends:

1. Create income generators that allow you to make enough money to fund charitable or research projects. Example: Bill Gates and the Bill & Melinda Gates Foundation.

2. Start a project or organization that creates global, national, or local solutions and seek donations to fund them. Example: Clara Barton and the American Red Cross.

3. Join projects and movements that are already established and help them in their fight. Example: NBA athletes and the NBA Cares.

4. Create for-profit companies that solve global issues. Example: DEKA Research & Development and the Slingshot.

5. Promote awareness for a cause you believe strongly in. Example: Lobbying or activism.

6. Get involved in the government and make changes to laws. Example: Shirley Franklin and Clean Water Atlanta.

Each one of these options will help you to lead a much richer and happier life than working a standard 9-to-5 job at X-Corp. Continue to educate yourself and become more aware of what's going on around you until you find the thing that excites you more than the rest.

Walking the Walk

There's nothing worse than a hypocrite, someone who says "Do this!" but doesn't follow his own advice. Many people can talk a good game, but they won't play one inning themselves.

Not me. In 2003, at the age of eighteen, I joined the U.S. Navy after high school in response to the attacks of 9/11. During my four years, I deployed twice on the USS Peleliu as a military police officer. My experiences gave me a much greater appreciation for the world's issues.

In 2005, I started volunteering with youth and single mothers at my local church. I linked up with a friend and began volunteering at a battered women's refuge for single mothers in Tijuana, Mexico, as well.

In 2007, I published my first two books to offer guidance to single-parent families raising boys. I traveled the country speaking and worked one-on-one with several families, nonprofits, and schools promoting education and social awareness.

In 2008, I started the S.T.R.O.N.G. Association, a nonprofit organization that serves youth and families around the country.

In 2010, I deployed to Afghanistan with the U.S. Army as a logistics officer in support of the war. My experiences there showed me there was a lot left to be done in developing global infrastructure to include logistics and construction.

In 2012, I started writing again and published the books you and your mother are reading now. I revived S.T.R.O.N.G. as well, this time with bigger ideas and plans.

Going forward, I have several ideas to increase financial literacy in America. One of them is the Millionaire Mind Youth Training Program. In addition, I have planned a yearlong global exploration tour for the purpose of studying global logistical supply chain challenges. During my travels, I hope to meet with local leaders around the world gathering ideas, data, and possible solutions I can compile into a uniform solution.

My current companies are profitable enough so that I can donate thousands of dollars a year to S.T.R.O.N.G. and other organizations fighting for change. I believe in what I'm telling you. I started off unaware, drunk, high, and unhappy. Today I'm involved, clear as a Texas sky, and excited about life, because I focused on a lifestyle design of income, influence, impact, and excitement.

Staying Up-to-date

There are thousands of websites that claim to have accurate news and information on the world's problems. Many of them are slanted to one view or another. To combat this problem, use the following four online resources to get your information:

StumbleUpon.com
StumbleUpon.com is an information website that allows you to pick areas that interest you and then with the click of a button provides awesome websites, news, and articles in that interest. This website can help you stumble upon your next big idea.

United Nations
The United Nations website (www.un.org) is a wonderful place to start learning about things going on in peace and security movements, human rights, humanitarian efforts, and international law. You can also jump directly to several other organizations, such as the World Health Organization.

TED (Technology, Entertainment, Design)
TED (www.ted.com) is a nonprofit devoted to "Ideas Worth Spreading." At their website you can join the conversations of some truly great minds on the subjects of technology, business, science, global issues, and more.

World Future Society
The World Future Society's website (www.wfs.org) is a goldmine of ideas on the future. The group's mission is to enable thinkers, political

personalities, scientists, and regular people to share an informed, serious dialogue on what the future will look like.

It's good to keep your ears and eyes focused on what's going on in the local and national news as well. When reading news, be careful not to let one media group's biases overly influence your opinions. I follow CNN, but I make sure to bounce any global news off other news agency websites such as the BBC, Associated Press (AP), Reuters, Al Jazeera, and others. This helps me to maintain a global picture versus just the American point of view.

Conclusion

After reading this book, there's probably no doubt in your mind about what you have to do.

- You have to get your family's life in order
- You have to start designing your life to meet your purpose
- You have to educate yourself
- You have to understand the world outside your neighborhood

The world is moving extremely fast. It seems like just yesterday we dreamed of flying cars. At the New York International Auto Show in April 2012, I saw the world's first flying car: the Terrafugia Transition. Now, we dream of turning ocean water into fuel and freshwater or using biogenetically engineered algae to power our cars.

Don't let society hold you back with its myths any longer. Don't remain passive and complacent any longer.

You have all you need to get started right between your ears.

Visit www.cedericktardy.com for the final video in the series. Video #8 titled *Create the Next Multibillion or Trillion Dollar Idea* will walk you through some of the changes taking place in the world and hopefully inspire you to create the next multibillion or trillion dollar idea of the future.

The Final Action Challenge

Your final action challenge is to go back and think over your lifestyle design ideas. Think about the lifestyle designs of your Dream Team and your friends. Do they encompass the progressive mindset? Are they big enough?

Challenge yourself to redesign the ideas you originally had so you're making the most of the opportunities available to you. Start this conversation with everyone around you.

I wish you the utmost success in all you do.

- Cederick

.

www.ingramcontent.com/pod-product-compliance
Lightning Source LLC
Chambersburg PA
CBHW071549040426
42452CB00008B/1117